AN ILLUSTRATED GUIDE TO
TANK BUSTERS

Bruce Quarrie　　**Mike Spick**

An Arco Military Book

PRENTICE HALL PRESS · New York

AN ILLUSTRATED GUIDE TO
TANK BUSTERS

A Salamander Book

Copyright © 1987 by Salamander Books Ltd.

All rights reserved, including the right of reproduction in whole or in part in any form.

An Arco Military Book

Published in 1987 by Prentice Hall Press
A Division of Simon & Schuster, Inc.
Gulf + Western Building
One Gulf + Western Plaza
New York, NY 10023

PRENTICE HALL PRESS is a trademark of Simon & Schuster, Inc.

Originally published in 1987 in the United Kingdom by Salamander Books, Ltd.

This book may not be sold outside the United States of America and Canada.

Contents

Introduction	10	AT-5 Spandrel	68
Aircraft	22	AT-6 Spiral	69
Fairchild A-10A Thunderbolt II	30	Belouga	70
Sukhoi Su-25 Frogfoot	32	BGM-71	70
Agusta A 129 Mangusta	34	CRV 7	72
Bell AH-1S HueyCobra	34	Folgore	72
MBB Bö 105 PAH-1	36	GBU-15 (V)	74
McDonnell Douglas AH-64A Apache	38	HOT 1 & 2	74
		Hydra 70	76
Mil Mi-24 Hind	40	Low-Altitude Dispenser (LAD)	76
Mil Mi-28 Havoc	42	LAW 80	76
Westland Lynx AH-1	44	MAPATS	76
Missiles, Rockets, Air-launched Scatter Weapons	46	MILAN	78
		Mehrzweckwaffe Eins (MW-1)	78
AGM-65 Maverick	62	Oerlikon SNORA 81	80
AGM-114A Hellfire	64	Panzerfaust 3	80
Apache/CWS	64	Paveway II & III	82
APILAS	66	RBS56 BILL	83
AT-4 Spigot	67	Rockeye II Mk 20 Cluster Bomb	84

Credits

Library of Congress Cataloging-in-Publication Data

Quarrie, Bruce
  An illustrated guide to tank busters.

  (An Arco Military Book)
  "A Salamander book" —
  1. Antitank weapons. I. Spick, Mike.
  II. Title.
  III. Series
  UF628.Q37 1987 623.4 87-43028
  ISBN 0-13-451154-9

  10 9 8 7 6 5 4 3 2 1

First Prentice Hall Press Edition

Editors: Ray Bonds and Richard Williams
Designed by South Coast Studios
Typeset by The Old Mill
Printed in Belgium by Proost International Book Production, Turnhout

Authors: Bruce Quarrie is an authority on armoured warfare. His many books on the subject include *Panzers in Russia 1943-45*, *Tank Battles in Miniature*; *Arab-Israeli Wars since 1947*, and *The World's Elite Forces*.

Mike Spick is the author of several works on modern combat aircraft and the tactics of air warfare, including Salamander's *Modern Air Combat* and *Modern Fighting Helicopters* (both with Bill Gunston), as well as two companion volumes to this book, *An Illustrated Guide to Modern Fighter Combat* and *An Illustrated Guide to Modern Attack*

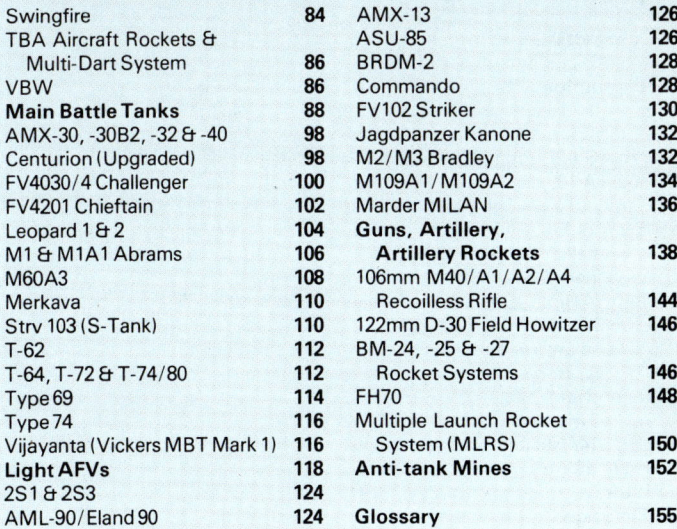

Swingfire	84	AMX-13	126
TBA Aircraft Rockets & Multi-Dart System	86	ASU-85	126
		BRDM-2	128
VBW	86	Commando	128
Main Battle Tanks	**88**	FV102 Striker	130
AMX-30, -30B2, -32 & -40	98	Jagdpanzer Kanone	132
Centurion (Upgraded)	98	M2/M3 Bradley	132
FV4030/4 Challenger	100	M109A1/M109A2	134
FV4201 Chieftain	102	Marder MILAN	136
Leopard 1 & 2	104	**Guns, Artillery, Artillery Rockets**	**138**
M1 & M1A1 Abrams	106		
M60A3	108	106mm M40/A1/A2/A4 Recoilless Rifle	144
Merkava	110		
Strv 103 (S-Tank)	110	122mm D-30 Field Howitzer	146
T-62	112	BM-24, -25 & -27 Rocket Systems	146
T-64, T-72 & T-74/80	112		
Type 69	114	FH70	148
Type 74	116	Multiple Launch Rocket System (MLRS)	150
Vijayanta (Vickers MBT Mark 1)	116		
Light AFVs	**118**	**Anti-tank Mines**	**152**
2S1 & 2S3	124		
AML-90/Eland 90	124	**Glossary**	**155**

Introduction

WHILE the modern main battle tank (MBT) is undoubtedly a formidable weapon, its true importance lies in its role as the spearhead of the combined arms land force. This is often overlooked, especially by those who have long forecast its demise as a battlefield weapon. While it is true that recent advances made in anti-tank weaponry have made the tank look very vulnerable, considerable advances have also been made in tank protection, not only in terms of improved armour, fire and explosion suppressants and the like, but in the tactical all-arms doctrine.

The MBT is accompanied into battle by mobile artillery and counter-air systems, and by motorised infantry riding in armoured personnel carriers (APCs). In this way it is accompanied by protective and supportive systems, which make the armoured force a far tougher nut to crack than if it was comprised of tanks alone. Further support comes from the air, from fixed- and rotary-wing aircraft; from long-range artillery; and from a comprehensive intelligence and reconnaissance system. Many of the misconceptions about the nature of armoured warfare arise from the particular scenario that the theorists see fit to concoct, often to demonstrate their preconceived ideas. Let us go back to basics for a moment.

A tank is essentially a mobile gun with good cross-country capability that is armoured to enable it to survive in relatively close proximity to the enemy. Tactics can reasonably be defined as the art of combining movement and firepower to the greatest discomfiture of the opponent, and the mobility and firepower of a modern MBT make it an excellent weapon. Armour and protective systems give it a measure of survivability, but this should not be confused with immortality. No tank has been, is, or ever will be, invincible.

Right: The basic Soviet field army is a homogenous force of armour, motorised infantry, artillery, and air support.

The tank can be attacked from the front, which is most likely, and this is where the heaviest armour is located; it can be attacked from the sides; aircraft can never entirely be prevented from working their way around to attack it from the rear where the protection is thinner; it can be attacked from the underside by mines; and finally, it can be attacked from the top, where the armour has always been thinnest, by an increasing number of weapons. Like any other weapon system, the tank is a compromise; adding protection adds

weight and reduces both mobility and range. Literally dozens of different weapons have the capability of knocking it out, and adequate protection against all of these is not possible. Finally, it is vulnerable to the 'mobility kill'; a tank with a track knocked off, the suspension broken, the motor out of action, or the turret jammed, is out of the battle as effectively as if it had been brewed up.

Knocking out tanks is relatively easy. The difficult bit is defeating a large-scale armoured thrust by a combined arms force, or overcoming a set-piece defensive position held by a similarly supported tank unit. As with so many other things, the whole is much greater than the sum of its parts. Having said that, the tank remains the pivot around which the combined arms unit hinges, and is thus a prime target.

Much depends on the scenario, and the one abiding interest is the 'worst case' conflict in Central Europe, where NATO forces are greatly outnumbered by their Warsaw Pact opposite numbers. The West has long tried to redress the ▶

TANK BUSTERS

balance with superior technology, but there can be no guarantee that this will necessarily prevail against good tactics backed by greatly superior numbers. Unless a technical advantage is backed by tactical superiority, any conflict will almost inevitably degenerate into a slogging match of attrition, and this is where numbers count.

This particular scenario has often been envisaged as a 'wall-to-wall' wave of Soviet armour driving across West Germany, backed by almost unlimited echelons coming up in support and taking over from the leading units when they have been hit hard, or even when they need to refuel and replenish. This is unlikely, since even the Soviet Union simply does not have these kinds of resources, formidable as their forces are. What then may we reasonably expect? The following extract is the view of Soviet Colonel F. Sverdlov, quoted in *Voyennyy Vestnik* No. 8, 1983.

> '... it is difficult to count on success without extensive manoeuvre. The expanded front of combat operations does not allow the assurance of equally high densities of forces and weapons everywhere, and makes it necessary to compensate for this deficiency by manoeuvre of units and fire. The importance of this will be even more obvious when examining typical features of modern combat, such as its decisiveness, speed of development, and great depth when the situation undergoes an abrupt change. Decisiveness of operations, which assumes boldness, initiative, and surprise in delivering attacks, is inconceivable without preliminary manoeuvre.'

From this we may assume that the Soviet Army will not, as is often supposed, keep rolling on like an unthinking juggernaut, without regard to losses. Rather it will be flexible, sustaining the speed of the advance by bypassing strongpoints and leaving them to be subdued by follow-on forces where this is possible, while switching the line of attack to concentrate overwhelming force where it is not. We must also remember that war is not a conflict between tanks and anti-tank weapons; it is an interplay between all the assets of one side against all the assets of the other. This is a truly formidable proposition; how will the tankbusters deal with it?

The problem devolves into two main areas; stopping the first echelon of the attack, and preventing follow-on forces from effectively reinforcing and taking over from it. We shall deal with each of these in turn. In passing, we must make a brief mention of the air battle which will be raging overhead, as this will directly affect the amount of force that can be brought to bear on the land battle. Successful attacks on enemy airfields will reduce the amount of close air support available to the commanders on the ground, as will the attainment of local air superiority in critical areas, which will enable strikes to be intercepted and disrupted, and will reduce or eliminate enemy air reconnaissance.

Stopping power

Stopping the first echelon, or at least slowing down the rate of advance, is obviously a primary task. The initiative will almost certainly lie with the attackers, and one of the first things to be done is to try to identify the main axis of the thrust, and its strength. The defences can then be arranged accordingly, to meet it in the most effective manner. Close air support will probably be called up immediately if suitable units are based near enough to react quickly, although the fast-mover jets will almost certainly be based a long way back.

Defence and battlefield control become much simpler if you know where the enemy is, and where he appears to be going. It is also necessary to be able to discern which are the main thrusts and which are feints. Reconnaissance is therefore essential. The view from the ground is too limited, while satellites are also for various reasons, including the weather, too restricted. The broad picture is built up from a number of sources, which include fast-mover jets, communications monitoring, and remotely piloted vehicles (RPVs). Currently under development is the joint surveillance target attack radar system, usually known

INTRODUCTION

Above: This Lynx is using an underslung DAT dispenser to lay an anti-tank/anti-personnel minefield from the air.

as Joint STARS. This is a Boeing E-8A fitted with synthetic aperture radar capable of detecting both slow-moving and stationary tanks and armoured fighting vehicles (AFVs) at a distance of up to 255 miles (408km); this information is passed back to the ground via digital data link. A modified Boeing 707 airliner, it will be too vulnerable to operate close up to the front line of troops (FLOT), a fact which reduces its effective range.

A deployed Soviet armoured division occupies an area some 6 miles (10km) wide and 19 miles (30km) deep. The leading echelon consists of tanks and APCs supported by self-propelled guns (SPGs), mobile surface-to-air missiles (SAMs), and radar-laid guns in the form of the formidable ZSU-23/4. Behind is a screen of rather longer-ranged SAMs, probably the SA-11 Gadfly, which can provide cover to the leading units. Behind this again is a second wave of AFVs and air-defence assets, again screened by longer-ranged SAMs. Armed helicopters such as the Hind will probably be used to scout along the front and flanks, and suppress such ▶

TANK BUSTERS

defences as they can find, while fixed-wing close air support units will range ahead. This combination presents a formidable multi-layered defence.

Once the main line of advance is identified, the priority becomes to select a suitable killing-ground. This is in essence an area with plenty of cover, backed by good access and egress routes (in case a retreat becomes necessary), fronting an open area which the attacking force will have to cross. If time permits, this can be liberally sown with mines, which can be dispensed either by a mechanical layer, or air-dropped by fixed-wing aircraft or by helicopters, or laid by medium-range rockets carrying them as submunitions, or by artillery shells. Mine fuzes are becoming increasingly clever, using seismic, magnetic, infra-red (IR), or acoustic sensors, and can be reliably programmed to detonate beneath the centre third of an AFV. Some can even discriminate between tracked and wheeled vehicles.

As the attacking force comes into range, it will be subjected to an artillery barrage. Many of the shells will dispense top-attack munitions; others will be laser-guided onto individual targets. Even the 'dumb' high-explosive (HE) shells will serve a useful purpose; a direct hit on an MBT will do it no good at all, while a hit on an APC will be devastating. Fragments, while unlikely to damage tanks, may prove lethal against the lighter armour, while even the MBTs will be forced to 'button up', which reduces their situational awareness and makes them less effective. Where 'smart' weapons are used, from whatever source, there are two priority targets. These are the command and communication vehicles, which can generally be identified by their groupings, and the mobile air defences. If the command structure can be knocked out, the force rapidly becomes disorganised and less effective, while the more air-defence assets are eliminated, the more effective the close air support will be.

The tankbusting MBT

The tank is itself an effective anti-tank weapon. Ensconced in a concealed, hull-down position, with only its turret showing, it has a great advantage over its counterpart caught in the open, moving, and half-blinded by the dust and smoke of the artillery barrage. Under these circumstances it can enjoy the luxury of a toe-to-toe slugging match with enemy tanks, a risk which no other weapon system can take. However, since it remains vulnerable to artillery fire, air attack, and counter-attack by missile-armed infantry, it still represents only a part of the whole tank-busting operation.

Below: This Swedish-made RBS56 BILL missile gives the infantryman a formidable anti-tank capability.

Also on the ground are the various anti-tank missile systems. These include the unguided rocket with a disposable launcher carried by one man in addition to his personal weapons, with an effective range of about 1,000ft (300m), as well as the guided missiles, often mounted on vehicles, with a range of up to 2.5 miles (4km). The former gives the infantryman an anti-armour protection capability at close range, and is particularly suited to urban fighting, where hard cover is plentiful and visibility is limited, although it is equally useful in close country. Many of these short-ranged weapons can be set up as mines, automatically triggered by a target that blunders through their line of fire. The longer-ranged guided weapons can be sited in a defensive position overlooking the killing-ground. Many of them can be launched from a remote sighting position, which gives a measure of security to the operator if the launch position is spotted and counterfire put down, while with some systems, up to six missiles, on six different sites, can be linked to one remote firing position. The vehicle-mounted missiles are slightly different; two or three launches, and the vehicle must change position before the counterfire comes raining down.

Helicopter ambush

One of the most deadly anti-tank weapons is the battlefield helicopter. The Soviet Union appears to regard it as a shock weapon, to be used in conjunction with the all-arms land force, but in the West it is considered to be a weapon of ambush, specifically in the anti-tank role. This seems to be the correct usage, as despite recent attempts to make battlefield helicopters more robust, they remain extremely vulnerable even to smallarms fire. Tactics are of course variable, but let us take as an example the methods of the British Army Air Corps.

The minimum number of attack helicopters in a formation is three, but as many as three squadrons may be used on one mission. They are accompanied by a minimum of two unarmed scout helicopters. Once tasked, the outbound leg is flown nap-of-the-earth (NOE) to avoid the attentions of enemy fighters. When within 9 miles (15 km), they get right down among the cabbages and hover-taxi forward, using every bit of cover possible, until they reach a 'measle', a predesignated area so-called because it is marked in pink on their maps. They then sit on the ground with engines running while the scouts creep carefully forward to assess the situation, which may have changed since the mission was briefed.

Both the killing-ground and the ambush positions will have been preselected. The ideal ambush position is one behind rising ground in a position where the helicopter will not be silhouetted against the sky. The attack helicopters will not be called forward to their ambush positions until the enemy force is nearing maximum missile range. Signals are exchanged between machines by means of flash cards, each with a large letter on it, which conform to a prearranged code. This cuts radio transmissions to a minimum and enables the unit to work in the face of heavy jamming. With all machines in position, missiles armed and targets selected, the initial launch is simultaneous. Target priority is also command vehicles and counter-air units, perhaps with more accent on counter-air units, for obvious reasons. The attack is best launched on the flank of the target array. Missile time of flight to maximum effective range will be something over 15 seconds. At most, four missiles will be launched from each helicopter before pulling back to the next measle, ready to repeat the attack from a different position. This is because their position will have been located and they will come under fire if they stay put. They are, however, tremendously difficult to see when in ambush because the sight is roof-mounted, and only the sight and the rotor protrude from cover; the missile launch and flight are almost impossible for the target to detect.

After the attack helicopter, the machine most likely to have a great influence over the battlefield is the slow-mover jet, of which there are only two types in service; the Soviet Frogfoot and the American Fairchild A-10A. As we do not know how ▶

TANK BUSTERS

▶ the Soviets intend to use Frogfoot, we must concentrate on the A-10A. It was designed as a survivable, although not immortal, tankbusting aircraft, with an enormous gun and smart missiles. Unlike the fast-mover jets, it is designed to operate without overflying the target array, and its low speed and high manoeuvrability allow it to attack and turn away very quickly; the smart missiles are 'launch-and-leave' Mavericks. Target identification can be a problem, even at speeds as low as the A-10A customarily uses. To overcome this, elements of A-10As are given specific areas to work, and they try to emerge from friendly territory at low level and egress the same way. Laser designation helps, although the troops on the ground are sometimes a little chary of using it, as it can betray their own position. Basically, identification, as with the helicopters, has to be visual, although on exercises another method has been found to work. If friendly helicopters can be seen in ambush positions, it is a fair assumption that the armoured array in the distance is hostile. While there is no direct liaison between fixed- and rotary-wing craft, it has been found that their mutual presence on the battlefield increases the total effect out of all proportion to their numbers, as each serves to distract the defences from each other. An A-10A is expected to kill rather more than four tanks per sortie, while exercises have shown that 19 tanks are killed for each helicopter lost.

Fast jets using scatter weapons such as cluster bomb units (CBUs) or dispensers can also play a useful anti-tank role in the battle area, but ideally they are best employed further over into hostile territory. Many weapons can be deployed against the leading enemy echelons, but the follow-on units coming up from behind tend to be far more vulnerable.

The MBT is heavy, rather slow, and often unreliable. The rule of thumb for tank movement is that for every 62 miles (100km) travelled, about one-third of the force will suffer a breakdown of some sort. It is fairly essential that tanks do not have to move too far under their own steam before reaching the battle area

HEAT rounds
A jet of molten metal pierces armour. Penetration depends on warhead diameter, not velocity.

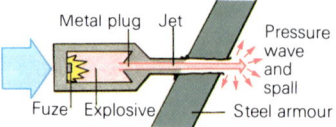

HESH rounds
Crumple on impact, then detonate. Shock waves detach scabs of armour inside tank.

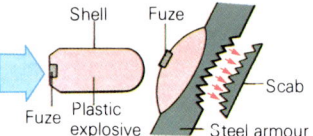

APDS rounds
Have dense metal core inside a sabot which is discarded as the round leaves the barrel.

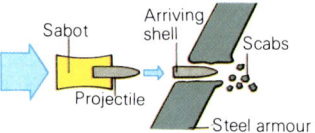

Chobham armour
A material of secret composition claimed to protect against HEAT, HESH and APDS rounds.

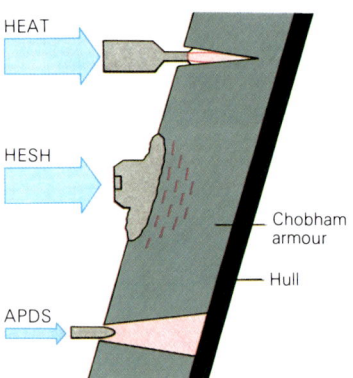

Reactive armour
Explodes when hit by AT rounds. This dissipates the jet of HEAT, and may deflect APDS rounds.

INTRODUCTION

if they are to preserve their mobility, and this means that they need to be brought up either by rail or by transporter. Rail is by far the most efficient means, but it is also the most easily interdicted. Transporters are less vulnerable, but they demand a tremendous logistics effort, and are dependent on hard roads. Roads have choke points, places where they are restricted by terrain, or bridges, or built-up areas, or simply by several roads all going in roughly the same direction coming together, with an ensuing traffic snarl-up. Choke points are favourite places for air attack because they are so vulnerable; if a route is blocked, the vehicles back up and become excellent targets.

Armoured or motorised divisions demand a colossal amount of stores to keep them going; tanks without fuel, lubricants or ammunition become liabilities rather than assets. Without reinforcements and supplies, an armoured thrust simply grinds to a halt. While fast jets can be armed to operate in the anti-tank role, it is in the interdiction mission that they have the greatest effect, albeit indirectly. It is also relevant to ask if, in the battle zone, it is worth risking a multi-million-dollar aircraft in an attack on a relatively cheap tank, bearing in mind that the tank is heavily protected against air attack, and that few of the weapons carried by a fast jet give much of a chance of a direct hit, which is what is needed to destroy an MBT.

Ammunition v protection

Tank development has always been a contest between ammunition and protection. At one time it was simply a matter of improving guns on the one hand and thickening the armour on the other. In recent years, with the advent of composite and reactive armour, it has become increasingly difficult to know which is winning the contest. There can be no doubt that manufacturers' claims are sometimes overstated on both sides. In two decades or so we may know the truth.

There are currently three main types of anti-armour warhead in use today. These are the shock-wave-inducing high-explosive squash head (HESH); the brute force kinetic energy penetrator (KEP), of which the self-forging fragment is the latest manifestation; and the molten-metal jet of the hollow charge, also frequently known as the shaped charge. These warheads are propelled towards the target by guns, by rocket motors, and sometimes simply dropped from above. They can be both guided and unguided.

HESH missile

The HESH warhead contains a large amount of plastic explosive in a soft container; on impact this spreads onto the face of the armour where it is detonated by a fuze. The resultant explosion sends a shock wave through the armour and flakes off large scabs of metal on the inside at high velocity which ricochet around the interior of the tank, cutting through everything in their path, including the crew. Effective against homogenous armour, it is less so against modern composites. An experimental missile was developed with a HESH head, but the quantity of explosive needed was so large that the missile was enormous, and development ceased.

The KEP is the time-honoured anti-tank round, designed to punch its way through armour. The formula for kinetic energy is ½ mass x velocity^2; having achieved the highest possible combination of mass and velocity, it needs to be applied to the smallest possible area for the greatest penetration to be achieved. Tungsten carbide is the most widely used penetrator material, but in recent years depleted uranium has gained in popularity, being cheap, very dense, and easily available. It has the further advantage as an anti-tank warhead of being pyrophoric, self-igniting on impact to release a tremendous amount of heat and brilliant white light. It is not a new development, being used by the Wehrmacht from 1944 onwards after tungsten supplies were cut off. Nor has depleted uranium any sinister qualities, being sufficiently innocuous to be used in civil airliner applications. It is used in the 30mm shells of the giant GAU-8/A aircraft gun carried by the A-10A, in many other anti-tank shells, and is ▶

TANK BUSTERS

▶ proposed for use in the new Hyper-Velocity Missile (HVM).

One way of increasing the effect of a KEP round is to use a sub-calibre projectile of dense metal held in a discarding sleeve — the armour-piercing discarding sabot (APDS) round. The sabot is discarded as the round leaves the barrel of the gun. It is, like so many other projectiles, spin-stabilised; the law of conservation of angular momentum keeping it spinning on its own axis through its own inertia. This has a flaw, in that the length/diameter ratio must not exceed 5:1. To achieve a greater l/d ratio, and thus a projectile with greater mass with no sacrifice of the slim diameter, fin stabilisation must be used. The resulting long-rod penetrator is called the armour-piercing fin-stabilised discarding sabot (APFSDS) round, which is in widespread use today.

The latest KEP projectile is the self-forging fragment, which consists of a metal disc which is formed into a hyper-velocity projectile by an explosive pressure wave. Still in the advanced development stage, this appears very promising, although details of its penetrative capabilities have yet to be released, and it appears to be very reliant on achieving the correct stand-off distance for detonation.

The hollow-charge high-explosive anti-tank (HEAT) round is in very widespread use in all forms of shell and missile. Dating from the 1940s, it consists of a cone-shaped charge of HE, which, detonated at the correct stand-off distance, can burn through armour to a considerable depth, in some cases, the manufacturers claim, more than 39in (1m). The actual penetration distance is closely related to the charge diameter and is not dependent upon the impact velocity, although certain reservations need to be considered. First, maximum penetration is achieved by the missile detonating at the optimum stand-off distance, and the test is carried out under static conditions. The dynamic conditions of the battlefield are likely to be less than ideal, with a consequent reduction in performance. Secondly, very deep penetration is achieved at the expense of the size of the perforation; if the hole is small and the residual energy low, little damage will be done to the interior of the tank. A

INTRODUCTION

rough guide is that lethal effect only begins to be obtained at a penetration distance of some 8in (200mm) less than the maximum. Thirdly, armour designers have not stood still; modern composite armour is reckoned to be a minimum of 2½ times more effective than the homogenous variety, while reactive armour is intended to disrupt the jet from the hollow charge. Finally, the angle at which the warhead strikes the target is important, as anything less than the optimum (90 degrees) not only effectively increases the armour thickness, but renders the jet less potent. This is further compounded by the fact that missiles, flying partially if not wholly on body lift, tend to assume a nose-up attitude.

On the other hand, hollow-charge warheads lend themselves readily to top attack where the protection is thinnest, and apart from their use in free-fall submunitions, can be angled downwards, as in the Swedish RBS 56 BILL missile, which is currently setting a trend. A further trend which is still in its early stages is the use of multiple hollow charges, the first setting off any reactive armour, and weakening composite armour before the second detonates a moment later.

The ultimate anti-tank weapon is of course nuclear. A medium-sized weapon could easily take out an entire armoured division, while a small tactical weapon could make a nasty mess of a regiment. Means of delivery are almost infinite: artillery shells, free-fall bombs, cruise missiles, and of course the battlefield support rocket, of which the Soviet Union has a great many. The West also has its share, of which the French Pluton is fairly representative. Mounted on an AMX-30 tank chassis for mobility, Pluton weighs just under 2.5 tons, is 25ft (7.64m) long, and has a diameter of 2.13ft (650mm). A solid fuel rocket, it has a maximum range of about 75 miles (120km), and uses strapdown inertial guidance. Either a 15 or a 25kT warhead is carried. It is to be replaced in the 1990s by Hades, which has double the range.

Going nuclear

Nuclear weapons release their energy in the form of heat, blast, radiation, and electro-magnetic pulse (EMP). Disregarding the effects (devastating and incalculable), of lingering radioactive fall-out, a relatively small weapon of some 10 kT will cause tremendous destruction over an area of about 80 square miles (200 sq.km), and the collateral damage will be horrendous. On the other hand, it is just possible that the crew of an MBT, protected in their metal carapace, will survive at quite close ranges to the point of detonation, called ground zero, although their vehicle would be immobilised. Is it realistic to consider the use of such weapons? Colonel Sverdlov, quoted earlier, is quite explicit.

'By employing nuclear weapons, it is possible to inflict decisive damage on the enemy, create breaches and gaps in formations, and allow units to make a swift manoeuvre and advance into the openings, all in the shortest possible time.'

The theoretical (no-one has ever ▶

Left: The French Pluton rocket roars away from its carrier, bound for a distant target.

TANK BUSTERS

▶ done it for real) tactics of nuclear warfare are well known: avoid large troop concentrations, switch the line of attack often and unpredictably, concentrate force only in the vicinity of the enemy, and close with him quickly. Use the fringes of irradiated areas to cross and outflank. Above all, use nuclear weapons to take out those of the enemy. A variation on this theme looks set to take its place in the scheme of things following broad hints that France may have begun production of the Enhanced Radiation Weapon (ERW), more commonly known as the neutron bomb. Rather ludicrously hailed by the popular press in the late 1970s as the 'bomb that kills people but spares property', the ERW releases about 80 per cent of its energy in the form of fast neutrons, which no armour can stop. As a result, a 1kT ERW would be more lethal against the personnel of an armoured force over a wide area than the previously mentioned 10kT weapon while restricting the heat and blast damage, and with it collateral damage and civilian casualties, to a comparatively small area. Considerable alarm has been raised about the deployment of this weapon, as it makes the use of tactical nuclear weapons much easier, and it is argued that this makes it far more likely to be used. A high-ranking French officer has stated, although not officially, that the ERW would only be used against an invader who already stood on French soil; there could therefore be no argument about collateral damage being caused in the country of an ally. This seems reasonable, if a little late in the day.

Possible anti-tank weapons of the future include fuel-air explosives (FAE), lasers, directed-energy weapons, and battlefield robots. Of these, the FAE already exists, and saw limited use in Vietnam. The FAE weapon is an attempt to simulate the

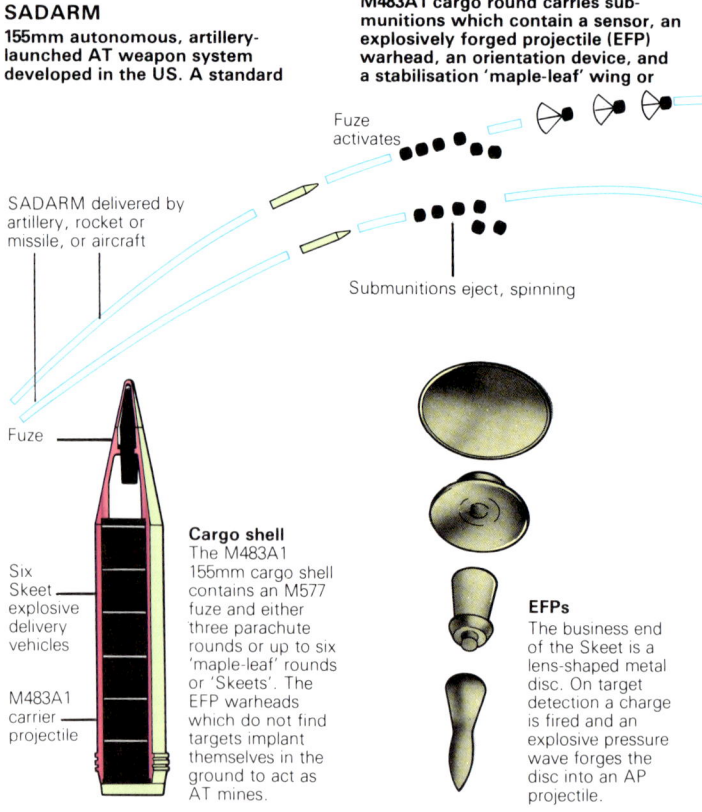

SADARM
155mm autonomous, artillery-launched AT weapon system developed in the US. A standard

M483A1 cargo round carries sub-munitions which contain a sensor, an explosively forged projectile (EFP) warhead, an orientation device, and a stabilisation 'maple-leaf' wing or

Fuze activates

SADARM delivered by artillery, rocket or missile, or aircraft

Submunitions eject, spinning

Fuze

Six Skeet explosive delivery vehicles

M483A1 carrier projectile

Cargo shell
The M483A1 155mm cargo shell contains an M577 fuze and either three parachute rounds or up to six 'maple-leaf' rounds or 'Skeets'. The EFP warheads which do not find targets implant themselves in the ground to act as AT mines.

EFPs
The business end of the Skeet is a lens-shaped metal disc. On target detection a charge is fired and an explosive pressure wave forges the disc into an AP projectile.

INTRODUCTION

massive destruction wrought by an explosion in a chemical factory in a controlled manner. The principle is simple. Volatile fuel gases or droplets are mixed with the air to form a cloud, which is ignited when the correct fuel/oxygen ratio has been reached. Unfortunately, the clouds are at the mercy of the local weather conditions, and the results tend to be a little wayward. If done correctly, a tremendous overpressure is created, which moves out from the centre at only marginally subsonic speeds, flattening everything in its path. While this is the same effect as ordinary HE, much greater results can be achieved. The US Navy is believed to have a weapon under development that weighs only 1,000lb (454kg) which can generate an overpressure of 8lb/sq.in (5.62 tonnes/m^2) out to a distance of 600ft (183m). This is more than enough to destroy the optical kit of a tank. For the future, if it can be perfected, the advantage against tanks lies in the fact that the aerosol cloud can seep into them, the resultant explosion destroying them from the inside. The FAE may well supplant the tactical nuclear weapon at some future point as a weapon of massive area destruction, but without the radiation hazards.

Lasers and robots

Directed-energy weapons break down into lasers and particle-beam weapons, and neither poses much of a hazard to the tank at present, unless lasers are used to blind the crew. Progress to date is that lasers can cut through metal under factory conditions at a range of a few inches, while airborne lasers have been used to knock down drones and missiles. These are very flimsy compared to a tank.

Battlefield robots present far more immediately useful possibilities. They range from remotely controlled tanks to airborne drones to unmanned battle stations. The choice is vast, but surely one of the most interesting is the Grumman Ranger, which commenced range testing in June 1985.

Ranger is small, weighing just 380lb (172kg), quiet, powered by electric motors, mobile, capable of 10 mph (16km/h) and low-slung, about 3ft(1m) high. The chassis is diamond-shaped with a wheel on each corner, and capable of carrying a payload of two Apilas anti-tank weapons, a 7.62mm machine-gun, a teargas launcher, and even a 12-bore shotgun. Unlike so many previous weapons, it is not a line-of-sight (LOS) vehicle, but truly remote. It is linked by fibre optics to the control console, which has a video screen on which the operator can see everything within the view of Ranger's scanning TV camera. In ambush, it can be switched to a 'listen only' mode, and if a target is detected, will warn the operator with an audible tone. Constant monitoring of the screen is thus not necessary. Ranger is also remote, with an operating range stated to be 6 miles (10km). It has been successfully controlled by troops with no previous experience and minimal instruction. This certainly seems to be a tankbusting weapon with a future.

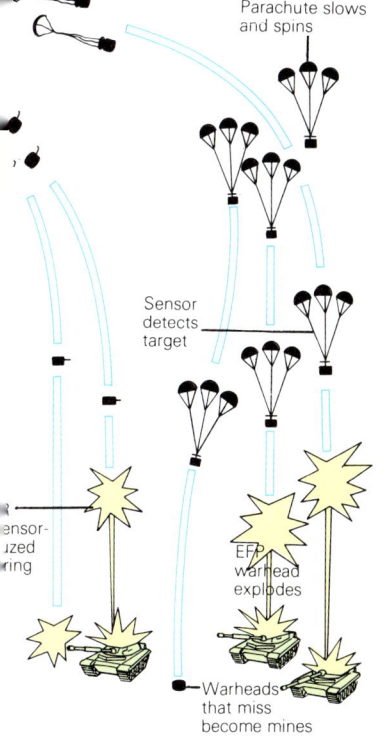

parachute. The submunitions are base-ejected over the target and then spin down. On detecting a target the EFP warhead is fired at the vulnerable top armour.

Parachute slows and spins

Sensor detects target

EFP warhead explodes

Warheads that miss become mines

Aircraft

AIR POWER represents flexibility over the battlefield that is impossible to achieve in any other way. In sheer speed of response it is unmatched. Only air power gives the ability to use the same assets in precision attacks on battlefield targets maybe hundreds of miles apart within a matter of hours. However, it is not a panacea for all ills; air power has its strengths, but it also has its limitations. Perhaps its greatest weakness is its comparative inability to operate as effectively in darkness or adverse weather as it can in daylight and clear skies. Ground forces are also disadvantaged by these conditions, but to nowhere like the same extent.

As we saw in the introduction, the battlefield scenario is not just a question of anti-tank systems versus tanks; it is an all-arms conflict. Tanks do not enter the battle unsupported; they operate in conjuction with their close-air-support aircraft, artillery, motorised infantry, and air defence systems consisting of both guns and missiles. It is against this background that we must examine the role of anti-tank aircraft, including helicopters.

The amazing range of modern weaponry permits almost any aircraft to be equipped for anti-tank operations, although few of them are really effective. Not only do they have to find the target and hit it, but they must be able to survive the enemy fighters and ground-based counter-

Two fixed-wing aircraft and several helicopters are operated as dedicated tank-destroyers.

air systems. To find the target, they need both accurate intelligence and accurate navigation systems, or alternatively, a very sophisticated sensor suite. At the most basic level, what is needed are sharp-eyed pilots and luck.

To hit the target, and what we are talking about is an armoured formation, and not a solitary tank, the right weapon for the circumstances is needed, together with an accurate aiming system. Survival is a combination of speed, manoeuvre, good flying and teamwork, countermeasures, and concealment, and, if the weapons carried confer a stand-off capability, this is also a decided advantage, as overflying a modern tank force with its supporting counter-air vehicles is a poor insurance risk, especially in daylight and clear weather.

Three types of flying machine will be tasked with anti-tank operations. These are: the fast movers, tactical jet fighters flying at low level and high subsonic speeds; the slow movers, of which only two types are known to exist; and rotary-wing types, i.e., helicopters.

The fast movers are too numerous to list, and little point would be served by it as they have many other functions which will often be considered more important. They will

Below: The Luftwaffe Tornado with the MW-1 dispenser is a potent anti-armour system.

TANK BUSTERS

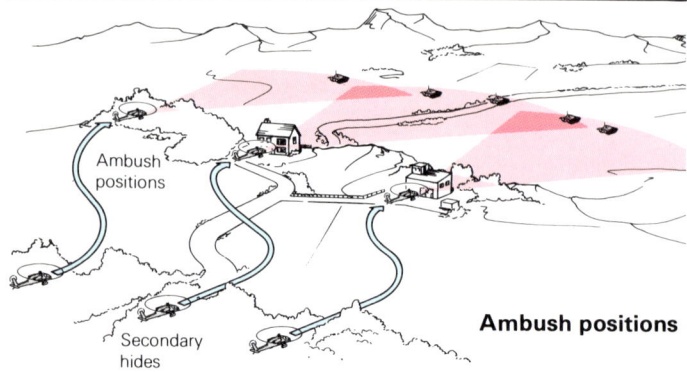

Ambush positions

Above: Three attack helicopters move up to ambush positions from their secondary hides only at the last minute. To launch a missile (below), they break cover with a pop-up or pop-sideways movement.

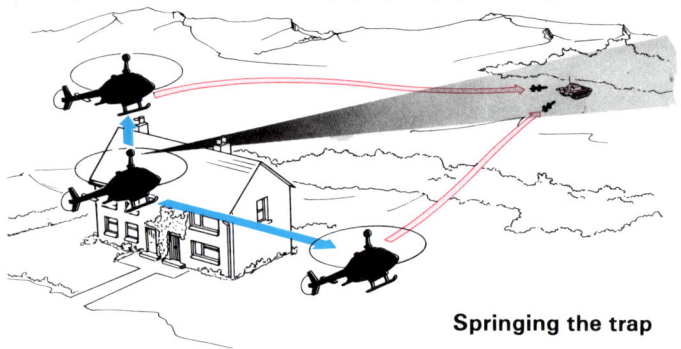

Springing the trap

▶ survive over the battlefield by using a combination of speed and low-flying, giving the enemy air defences just the briefest window through which to strike back at them. As a generalisation, their speed is such that they have little time to aim, and virtually no time to make any but the smallest adjustments to their flight path to line up on target. Success will be due to their ability to come in from precisely the right direction at exactly the right time. Overflying the enemy battle array is impossible to avoid, and the most effective weapons for this form of attack will

Fixed-wing Slow-mover Aircraft

Name	Origin	Length ft(m)	Span ft(m)	Height ft(m)	Max. TO weight lb (kg)	Max. extl load lb(kg)	Hard-points
A-10A Th		53.33 (16.26)	57.50 (17.53)	14.67 (4.47)	50,000 (22,680)	16,000 (7,258)	11
Su-25 Frogfoot	USSR	49.22 (15.00)	46.90 (14.30)	16.41 (5.00)	40,000 (18,144)	12,000 (5,443)	10

Both aircraft have good short field performance, endurance, and manoeuvrability.

AIRCRAFT

Above: The STOVL Harrier can be based at forward locations, reducing its response time.

probably be those that scatter anti-tank submunitions over a broad pattern, either using dispensers or cluster bomb units (CBUs). This will give the best chance of knocking out one or two tanks on each run. The attack will probably be made in waves of up to four aircraft, from different directions, in swift succession. Other weapons can be used in this form of attack, such as pods of unguided rockets, although these will depend on individual targets coming beneath the aircraft's 'death dot', or continuously computed impact point (CCIP) during the run.

The aircraft cannon may be used to good effect against the lightly armoured personnel carriers, or air defence weapons, should any of them get in the way, but may not do much damage to an MBT.

Just two fast movers are especially worthy of note. The Tornado IDS, with its incredibly accurate nav/attack system, terrain-following system, and ability to deliver accurate first-pass blind attacks at night and in weather unfit for birds, ▶

Max. speed	Internal gun	Primary AT weapons	Secondary AT weapons
Mach 0.59	30mm GAU-8/A	AGM-65 Maverick	LGBs, CBUs, Unguided rockets in pods
Mach 0.74	30mm twin barrel?	AT-6 Spiral	LGBs, CBUs, Unguided rockets in pods

TANK BUSTERS

Rotary-wing Aircraft

Name	Origin	Role	Length ft(m)	Rotor dia. ft(m)	Empty weight lb(kg)	Max. TO weight lb(kg)	Engines
A 129 Mangusta	Italy	AT	40.28 (12.26)	39.04 (11.90)	5,575 (2,529)	9,039 (4,100)	2xRR Gem 2
AH-1S Huey Cobra	USA	AT	44.58 (13.59)	44.00 (13.40)	6,479 (2,939)	10,000 (4,356)	1xT53-703
AH-64 Apache	USA	AT	48.17 (14.68)	48.00 (14.63)	11,015 (4,996)	17,650 (8,006)	2xT700-701
Bo 105 PAH-1	W. Germany	AT, multi-role	38.92 (11.60)	32.28 (9.84)	4,217 (1,913)	5,511 (2,500)	2x250 C50B
Mi-24 Hind E	USSR	multi-role	60.67 (18.50)	55.75 (17.00)	16,534 (7,500)	24,250 (11,000)	2x TV3-117
Mi-28 Havoc	USSR	AT	57.08 (17.40)	55.75 (17.00)	14,990 (6,800)	20,060 (9,100)	2x TV3-117
Lynx AH-1	UK	AT, multi-role	52.19 (13.16)	42.00 (12.80)	5,683 (2,578)	10,000 (4,356)	2xRR Gem 2

▶ will be a formidable adversary to the tank, and the Luftwaffe operate it carrying the MW-1 dispenser with anti-tank submunitions. The other is the Harrier, probably using CBUs. The Harrier has the unusual advantage of being able to use unorthodox bases far nearer to the front lines than any other fast mover, and thus has the fastest response time of any aircraft.

On the whole, however, the fast movers will be better employed against armour well behind the battle area, when it is moving up and before it can deploy, preferably at choke points where there is a tendency to bunching, and where very good targets may be found.

The slow movers are potentially much more effective than the fast movers (which is why we have featured them in detail later), as they are able to make attacks on individual targets with weapons optimised for the task, rather than sowing the landscape with submunitions in the hope that one or two out of hundreds will find a billet. Only two 'slow jets' have been built: the American A-10A Thunderbolt II, and the Soviet Sukhoi Su-25 Frogfoot.

What little is known about the Su-25 (see p.32) shows it to be a similar kind of aircraft in many ways to the A-10A. The slow speed and excellent flying qualities of the A-10A enable it to approach the battle area at very low level, hugging the contours and using the terrain for concealment (terrain masking). The general rule is that helicopters have the height band between the treetops and the ground, while the A-10A stays just above the treetops, but in a shooting war the A-10A will take advantage of every scrap of cover going, and its flight regime allows this to be done, although pilot fatigue is high. When the front line of troops (FLOT) is identified, the big bird pulls sharply up to about 700ft (213m), acquires a target, aims in just a few seconds, then either fires the gun or launches a missile, after which it goes into a diving turn for the safety of the ground. In this way it limits its exposure time, making it a very poor target for the ground defences. Even if it is hit, it can often survive.

Low-speed agility

Turn capability is a function of speed, and the low speed and good manoeuvrability of the A-10A allow it to turn very quickly in a small space. Target acquisition is visual, and can be made from the same distance regardless of whether the aircraft is a fast or slow mover. At the preferred fighting speeds of the A-10A, the

AIRCRAFT

Total SHP kW	Sust. speed mph (km/h)	Climb ft/min (m/s)	Hover ceiling ft(m)	Range miles(km)	Op. radius incl. loiter miles (km)	Primary AT weapons	Secondary AT weapons
1,904 (1,416)	190 (306)	2,090 (10.61)	7,840 (2,390)	n/a	63 (100)	8xTOW or 8xHOT or 6xHellfire	rockets
1,800 (1,339)	141 (227)	1,620 (8.23)	7,500 (2,286)	316 (507)	n/a	8xTOW or 8xHellfire	rockets 20mm M197 gun
3,392 (2,523)	186 (300)	2,500 (12.70)	10,200 (3,109)	428 (689)	n/a	16xHellfire	rockets 30mm Chain Gun
840 (625)	137 (220)	1,770 (8.99)	5,298 (1,615)	408 (657)	n/a	6xHOT or 8xTOW	rockets
4,400 (3,272)	186 (300)	2,953 (15.00)	7,218 (2,200)	n/a	100 (160)	4xAT-6 Spiral or 4xAT-3 Sagger	rockets 23mm gun, CBUS
4,400 (3,272)	200 (322)	n/a	n/a	n/a	148 (240)	8xAT-6 Spiral	rockets 30mm
1,904 (1,416)	190 (306)	2,480 (12.60)	10,600 (3,231)	336 (541)	n/a	8xTOW	rockets

pop-up takes less forward distance, as does the aiming time, while the turn away keeps it much further from ground fire than would be the case with a fast mover, the speed of which would to a great degree negate the stand-off capability of Maverick. The F-16 has been the yardstick against which manoeuvre capability in fighters has long been measured, but at low speeds, the A-10A out-turns it with ease. In many cases the A-10A can attack and turn away without ever coming within the lethal envelope of the ground-based air-defence systems.

Although specifically designed as a tankbuster, the A-10A would not be tasked against individual targets, but would be given a geographical area to work. As with all tactical fighters it operates in the basic pair, although sometimes more than one pair would be used in a formation. Attacks will be closely sequenced, with a pair coming from the same direction but on slightly different headings and staggered, to confuse the defences. While one aircraft concentrates on its attack, the other gives cross-cover and assumes responsibility for collision avoidance. As the first comes off target, the roles reverse.

The low speed and high manoeuvrability of the A-10A enable it to work effectively in visibility that would rule out a fast mover. If we take for example a target located in a valley bottom, with a low cloud base shrouding the tops of the hills along the sides, even assuming that a fast mover could get in there in the first place, its only way out is upwards into the cloud, losing contact with both the target and the ground, at the same time becoming vulnerable to radar-laid guns and surface-to-air missiles (SAMs). An A-10A, on the other hand, could turn within the confines of the valley in many cases, and stay beneath the cloud base.

Even lower and slower than the slow movers are the rotary-wing craft: the helicopters. The battlefield helicopter relies to a large extent on stealth and concealment, and achieves this by making use of every feature that the terrain has to offer. It should really be regarded as a high-speed surface vehicle with 100 per cent cross-country capability, so low does it fly. Its main armament is mainly wire-guided missiles with high subsonic speeds, although there are signs that the next generation will be faster launch-and-leave missiles.

Ambush tactics
The forte of the anti-tank helicopter is the ambush. The ground is recon-

TANK BUSTERS

noitred beforehand, often by a pair of scouting helicopters, and the ambush position chosen. It should not be on the skyline, should provide solid cover, and have an ingress path which cannot be observed. The attack machines only move up when necessary; prior to the attack, they wait in a suitable holding area, if possible on the ground with their engines idling. In the British Army Air Corps a minimum of three helicopters is used for the attack, and more if feasible. If possible, the attack position is selected on the flank of the advancing armour so as not to place the helicopters directly in the line of fire of the tanks. Targets are selected and the missiles launched. Missile time of flight is probably about 15 seconds in a typical case, after which another target is selected. By this time, it is probable that their presence has been discovered, and the enemy artillery is about to plaster the area, so the helicopters withdraw to a pre-arranged spot to regroup and prepare to repeat the dose.

Helicopters are often photographed hiding among the treetops, but this does not make an ideal firing position. A heavy shell hitting the trunk of a tree results in large lumps of timber flying about which constitute a very real hazard to the helicopter, even though it may be armoured.

The modern anti-tank helicopter is extremely agile, but it lacks speed and operational radius, which reduce its reaction speed. The Soviet Union seems to take a rather different view of helicopter operations from that of the West, regarding it more as a shock weapon, scouting ahead of the armour and protecting its flanks.

Systems are currently being developed to enable fixed-wing aircraft and helicopters to operate during the hours of darkness. Notable among these is the low-altitude navigation and targeting infra-red night system (LANTIRN), which is scheduled to be fitted to many US tactical aircraft, including the F-16, but the problem for helicopters is more intractable. Thermal imaging sights to enable the attack to be made at night are no problem; the difficulty lies in getting the helicopter to the ambush position through the maze of obstructions, trees, power lines, etc., without compromising its nap-of-the-earth (NOE) flying capability, which would be the case if it was forced to fly high enough to clear them. The Soviet Union has experimented with illuminated night operations using flares; what conclusions they have drawn are not known.

Cannon are widely carried by both fixed- and rotary-winged aircraft, and armour piercing (AP) ammunition of varying types is available. While it is true to say that they are ineffective against the frontal armour of a modern MBT, it is possible in some cases to breach the thinner top and rear armour, and with some cannon the side armour also. This apart, even the lighter guns have their uses in the anti-armour role in that they can force the crew to 'button up', thereby reducing their effectiveness, and also chew up quite badly the supporting vehicles, armoured personnel carriers (APCs), and mobile counter-air systems. Nor should the possibility of a mobility kill be overlooked; an MBT with a track blown off or its turret jammed is out of the battle for all practical purposes.

Tankbusting cannon

Airborne cannon are, like most weapons, a compromise, to be used for many purposes. The only one specifically designed for tankbusting is the American GAU-8/A, carried by the A-10A, and this is huge, roughly 19ft (5.8m) long, weighing as much as a small helicopter, and possessing a colossal recoil force. Aircraft shells rely on kinetic energy for penetration, and therefore need a high mass coupled with a high muzzle velocity, and preferably a high rate of fire to maximise the number of hits. All these factors combine to increase the size and weight of the gun, but, particularly in the case of helicopters, there are limits to what can be installed without hopelessly compromising performance.

Oddly enough, fast movers have a

Right: The most powerful gun ever carried on an aircraft is the 30mm seven-barrel GAU-8/A, which arms the A-10A.

AIRCRAFT

slight edge in hitting power as the aircraft velocity increases the projectile velocity, although the problems of acquiring a target and aiming accurately are compounded.

The GAU-8/A, the only specifically anti-tank gun for aircraft, has seven barrels and spits out projectiles weighing 15oz (425g) and having a depleted uranium core, at the rate of 70 per second, with a muzzle velocity of 3,225ft/s (985m/s). The 20mm M61A1 has six barrels, a rate of fire of 100 shells per second, a muzzle velocity of 3,400ft/s (1,036m/s), with a projectile weight of only around 3.5oz (100g). The British Aden and French DEFA by contrast are single-barrelled cannon and fire a shell weighing almost three times as much as that of the M61 but at a much slower rate, typically 23 per second at a muzzle velocity of 2,600ft/s (790m/s). Soviet aircraft guns tend to fire much heavier shells for the calibre than the West, with a comparable muzzle velocity, but at a slower rate.

A few cannon have been developed specifically for helicopter use. Representative of these are the 25mm Oerlikon KBA, which fires an armour-piercing discarding sabot projectile weighing 5.3oz (150g) at a rate of 10 per second at 3,600ft/s (1,100m/s), and the 30mm Hughes M230 Chain Gun, which has a slightly higher rate of fire but a lower muzzle velocity, with a considerably heavier projectile.

TANK BUSTERS

Fairchild A-10A Thunderbolt II

The A-10A was originally conceived as a survivable slow mover, capable of carrying a heavy load of ordnance to a distance of 230 miles (370km), at 25,000ft (7,620m), loitering for two hours at 5,000ft (1,520m) at that radius, making multiple attacks, then returning to base at high altitude with a 20-minute fuel margin. It was designed around the huge 30mm GAU-8/A cannon, (developed in parallel), which is effective out to a slant range of 4,000ft (1,220m) against tanks, and 6,000ft (1,830m) against light armour.

The survivability of fast movers over the battlefield is accomplished by using high speed and low altitude to reduce the surface-to-air defence system's window. The method adopted by Fairchild on the A-10A was to reduce the window by a combination of ultra-low flying and manoeuvrability, in this way reducing the exposure time to enemy fire to less than many fast movers could achieve. The low speed and exceptional handling qualities enable the A-10A to be flown very close to the ground, taking advantage of any available cover; after attacking it can turn away very quickly, which often keeps it out of the enemy lethal fire envelope altogether. However, it was recognised that, in the smoke and confusion of the battlefield, total avoidance of the counter-air systems was not

AIRCRAFT

possible, and from time to time it was going to take hits. It was therefore designed to be exceptionally survivable, able to return to base with half a wing, a tail section or one engine missing, and other severe structural damage. Great attention was paid to fire prevention, and the protection of hydraulic systems, while the pilot was surrounded by a titanium armour bathtub.

The A-10A has a total of 11 hardpoints under the wings and fuselage, of which a maximum of either nine or ten can be used at once. While all of these are capable of carrying ordnance, the two outers are now to carry a pair of AIM-9L Sidewinders apiece for air defence, while at least one other station will be used for an ECM pod. ALE-40 chaff and flare dispensers are built in. The main anti-tank weapon carried is the AGM-65 Maverick, in the A, B, or D versions. A Pave Penny laser target finder is routinely carried to allow the aircraft to work with designator teams.

First flight: YA-10 prototype 10 May 1972, production A-10A 21 October 1975. Only one variant built, although a two-seat night all-weather (NAW) version was converted from a pre-production aircraft but not adopted. Production ceased 1982. **Users:** USAF (AFRes, ANG).

Below: The A-10A Thunderbolt II was designed for survivability, operating in the European theatre. The most formidable anti-tank aircraft ever built, these examples from the 81st TFW based at RAF Woodbridge/Bentwaters are carrying the standard anti-tank loading of four AGM-65 Mavericks.

TANK BUSTERS

Sukhoi Su-25 Frogfoot

Frogfoot has many features in common with the A-10A and was almost certainly designed to meet a similar requirement, but in many ways it is a very different aircraft, in spite of the tendency in Western circles to 'mirror image' it. Like the A-10A it is a slow mover with a very high aspect ratio wing, has a good range/loiter performance, can lift a heavy ordnance load, and can operate from short, semi-prepared airstrips. It is also believed that, like the A-10A, it is heavily armoured, and can absorb a great deal of punishment, although the design is obviously not as optimised for this as the American aircraft, not having the twin tails and outboard engine pods. Nor has it been designed around a monster cannon; the gun carried has yet to be identified, but appears to be a 23mm or possibly 30mm multi-barrel type located under the cockpit floor and offset to port.

It is dimensionally slightly smaller than the A-10A, and carries a smaller maximum warload on ten hardpoints under the wings. The two engines are Tumansky R-13-300 turbojets, which are rather thirsty in the demanding slow speed, low-level regime, although Frogfoot has demonstrated a good level of endurance over Afghanistan. While less economical than the turbofans of the American aircraft, they provide a considerably better thrust/weight ratio, which implies a superior short field performance, better acceleration, and better sustained turn. It is known that Frogfoot is considerably faster than the A-10A, and its climb rate is believed to be better. Wing loading is probably comparable.

Frogfoot features the chisel nose associated with a laser ranger, marked target seeker, and possibly designator, and can carry laser-guided-bombs (LGBs), although these are not the main anti-tank weapons, which are believed to be the AT-6 Spiral, a radio command guided weapon which is smaller and less effective than Maverick. Cluster weapons can also be carried, as can pods of unguided rockets.

Like most Soviet aircraft, Frogfoot presents many riddles to the West. Its gestation period was long for such a simple aircraft, and it does not appear to be entering Soviet service in any great numbers, although it is being exported. It is

AIRCRAFT

likely to see action with the Iraqi Air Force against Iran by mid-1987, and this may answer some questions about it.
First Flight: believed 1977. Service entry about 1981. Operational in Afghanistan, 1982. Two seater rumoured but not as yet confirmed. **Users:** Czechoslovakia, Hungary, Iraq, USSR.

Above: Frogfoot is the nearest Soviet equivalent to the A-10A although it is arguably less capable than 'the Warthog'.

Below: Frogfoot has been used in the counter-insurgency role in Afghanistan. Performance is more sprightly than the A-10A.

TANK BUSTERS

Agusta A 129 Mangusta

The Mangusta (Mongoose) originated from an Italian Army requirement back in 1972 for a battlefield helicopter, but little progress was made until 1978. At first derived from the multi-role A 109A, it has been developed out of all recognition into a narrow-profile tandem-seat machine with stub wings. These serve the dual purpose of unloading the rotor at high forward speeds while providing mountings for the main armament. The pilot sits behind and above the gunner, and the large transparencies which give excellent vision are the angular flat surface type which reduce sun glint and thus aid stealth.

Two Rolls Royce Gem 2 Mk 1004D turboshaft engines provide the power, and drive the four-bladed rotor, which has elastomeric bearings and needs no lubricant. The entire machine has been designed to have minimal maintenance, with ease of access to all parts. The structure has been designed to resist smallarms fire up to 12.7mm, and is said to be remarkably tolerant against 23mm projectiles. Extensive use has been made of composites and metal honeycomb panels, and particular attention has been given to reducing both infra-red (IR) and noise signatures.

The baseline mission is to fly 62 miles (100km) to the battlefield, mainly in NOE flight which involves much zigzagging and is probably worth at least double in straight-line flight; then loiter for 90 minutes, with at least half this time spent in the fuel-consuming hover, and return to base with an adequate safety margin. Mangusta is agile, and has high g-load factors. Acceleration is 0 to 70mph (112km/h) in 10 seconds, but neither climb nor sustained forward speed are anything special by the latest standards, although apart from the ferry mission, forward speed is fairly irrelevant.

A further development of the Mangusta has been proposed. Called Tonal, it

Bell AH-1S HueyCobra

The HueyCobra has probably seen more active service than any other rotary-wing machine, having been extensively used in Vietnam, the Middle East, and in the early stages of the Iraq/Iran war. The HueyCobra was developed from the ubiquitous UH-1 Huey, which dated from 1956. The most radical change in configuration was the narrowed fuselage, with tandem crew seating, and wings on which to hang weaponry which also helped to unload the rotor in forward flight, although most of the dynamic parts remained the same. The first HueyCobra variant was the AH-1G, which was powered by a single Avco-Lycoming T53-13 turboshaft engine. The AH-1S has the -703 turboshaft, with nearly 30 per cent more power to drive its two-bladed rotor.

The pilot sits above and behind the co-pilot/gunner, and is generally responsible for launching the wing weapons. The co-pilot/gunner controls a universal chin turret which houses either a 20mm or 30mm cannon, and manages the sight system in the nose. He can also fly the machine and control the wing weapons in emergencies. The performance of the AH-1S is nothing very special, and by comparison with the Mangusta, for instance, it is underpowered. It is, however, rather larger than the Italian machine, and can carry a greater weapons load, although both its range and endurance are restricted. This is probably a reflection on the age of the original concept; in its day it was one of the best. In fact many of the AH-1S models are rebuilt -1Gs.

The greatest weakness of the HueyCobra is probably the nose-mounted sight, which by contrast with the roof-mounted sight, or, even better, the mast-mounted sight, forces it to expose itself completely when aiming and tracking a

Right: The final variant of the HueyCobra is the AH-1W, seen here in its new US Marine Corps camouflage in March 1986.

AIRCRAFT

will be an uprated version for the armed forces of Britain, Italy, Holland and Spain, able to carry out the scouting and anti-tank roles, and also anti-helicopter operations.

First flight (Mangusta): 11 September 1983.

Above: The Mangusta uses the now classic tandem seating with flat transparencies, and is resistant to smallarms fire.

---

tube-launched optically-tracked wire-guided (TOW) missile. It cannot take up a hull-down position and is consequently easier to detect and more vulnerable to return fire.

Probably the final variant in the series is the more capable AH-1W, which is in service with the US Marine Corps. More powerful, and longer-legged, the -1W is very expensive, and will eventually be replaced by a more 'state of the art' machine.

First flight: 7 September 1965. **Users:** Greece, Iran, Israel, Japan, Jordan, Morocco, Saudi Arabia, Somalia, Spain, USA (Army, Marines, Navy).

TANK BUSTERS

MBB Bö 105PAH-1

By comparison with the other helicopters in this section, the Bö105 looks quite pretty; it is also the smallest by a considerable margin, has a poor payload capacity, and, except for range, has the poorest performance. On the other hand, it is extremely sprightly at low level. It is unarmoured, but its small size and manoeuvrability will make it a difficult target.

The four-blade rotor is of the rigid type, with feathering hinges only, with a forged titanium hub holding the blades in roller bearings. Flexing and torsion is taken up by the glassfibre spar, while the leading edge is protected by a titanium strip. The power is supplied by two Allison 250 C50B turboshafts. The pilot and co-pilot are seated side by side, and there is a three-seater bench behind them.

The design is now over 20 years old, and in some ways shows its age. At the outset it was one of the most expensive small helicopters around, but this was primarily due to its having two engines. It has since proved a great success, and over 1200 have been built to date in four countries.

The normal armament for anti-tank work is either six HOT missiles or eight TOW, but a wide range of unguided rockets and guns can be, and are, in the service of some dozen user countries. Aiming is via a roof-mounted sight, which allows the Bö 105 to operate hull-down in ambush positions.

Studies have been going on for some considerable time to develop this potent little machine, mainly by the installation of much more powerful engines. This could be done without loss of range capability by utilising some of the cabin space to accommodate extra fuel, and the result should be greater speed and lifting capacity, improved altitude performance, and better acceleration. Other improvements could be made to the sensors, navaids, and communications kit. Much depends, however, on whether a customer can be found; the two main criticisms of the Bö 105 are its small size and its lack of survivability, while there are far too many helicopter designs chasing too few orders. It is beginning to seem unlikely that further development will take place.

First flight: 16 February 1967. **Users:** China, Holland, Indonesia, Malaysia, Morocco, Nigeria, Philippines, Sierra Leone, Spain, Sudan, Sweden, West Germany, with many other civil customers.

AIRCRAFT

Above: The Bö 105, seen here launching a HOT missile, is generally considered to be too small for the anti-tank role.

Left: A Bö 105 armed with eight TOW missiles. Note the roof-mounted sight for target acquisition from cover.

TANK BUSTERS

McDonnell Douglas AH-64A Apache

The Apache is currently the ultimate in anti-tank helicopters. Agile, long legged, survivable, and hard-hitting, it goes almost without saying that it is large (for a two-seater), heavy (almost double the empty weight of the Mangusta), and expensive (about three times the cost).

The AH-64A follows the accepted attack helicopter layout pioneered by the HueyCobra in having tandem seats, with the pilot behind and above the co pilot/gunner, and using flat transparencies to reduce glint. It is powered by two GE T700-701 turboshaft engines with 'black hole' IR suppression to the effluxes. The design encompassed both minimal maintenance and ease of access, and the structure is tolerant of both 12.7mm and, to a lesser degree, 23mm projectile strikes. The landing gear is a wheeled type, with non retractable long stroke legs, intended to cushion the impact in an uncontrolled descent.

Range on internal fuel is some 36 per cent better than the HueyCobra, while the weapon-carrying stub wings are plumbed for long-range ferry tanks. A non stop ferry range of 1,168 miles (1,880km) was demonstrated in the summer of 1986.

The Apache carries an unparalleled range of sensors for target location, tracking and attack, including laser rangefinder/designator and spot tracker, IR, and pilot night vision sensors, and extremely sophisticated navigation and communications kit together with a comprehensive countermeasures suite. There is no doubt that it can attack effectively at night, but it is doubtful whether it is capable of NOE flight in an area festooned with power cables.

Basic anti-tank armament consists of no fewer than 16 Hellfire missiles, which use laser guidance. This is double the number of missiles carried by most

Right: The Apache, shown here carrying eight Hellfires and two Hydra 70 rocket pods, also mounts the Hughes Chain Gun.

Below: An Apache test-launches the first production Hellfire.

AIRCRAFT

other types. TOW is an alternative. and the usual unguided rocket pods can be carried, as can air-to-air missiles for self defence. A 30mm M230 pivoting Chain Gun is mounted beneath the centre-line, remotely controlled to cover the entire field of view of the sighting system. The aiming sensors are, however, all grouped on the nose, and no attempt seems to have been made to use a roof-mounted sight or, even better, a mast mounting. To attack, the Apache can hardly avoid exposing itself unless Hellfires are launched on a target designated by other sources. While this is possible, it can hardly be relied upon.
First flight: 30 September 1975. **User:** US Army.

TANK BUSTERS

Mil Mi-24 Hind

The Hind was conceived as a battlefield helicopter with the primary mission of depositing an eight-man combat squad at a critical point behind the enemy lines. It would not of course attempt this singly, but in large numbers in order to deposit an effective ground force. As it obviously had to cross into hostile territory to do so, it also had to carry enough ground-to-air ordnance to suppress or breach the local defences. It therefore had to be large, with the accent on speed rather than manoeuvrability. Later, the priorities were changed to assault, and while the load-carrying capability was retained, the front end was considerably redesigned to suit the new mission. The result was inevitably a compromise, with the result that the most recent variants, the Hind D and E, are not really suited to fly the anti-tank mission as it is understood in the West.

The seating is the orthodox tandem layout with the pilot set above and behind the gunner, with the full width cabin further back still. The five-bladed rotor has metal blades and features simple articulation. This, combined with the large size and weight of the main body, tends to make the response to control inputs slow, and this is further aggravated by the large stub wings which interact with the downwash from the rotor, with the result that the Hind is not really suited to

AIRCRAFT

Western-style NOE flight. On the other hand, the two IR-suppressed Isotov TV3-117 turboshaft engines drive the Hind faster in level flight than any other military helicopter currently in service, and at high speeds, the stub wings unload the rotor by an appreciable amount.

Operationally, the Hind seems to be used as an offensive rather than an ambush weapon. The favoured method is believed to be from a relatively high altitude with a steep diving attack at maximum effective weapons range. While this profile makes it vulnerable to ground-fire, it is heavily armoured; using speed rather than stealth also has advantages in open areas where cover does not exist. Hind is also used to range along the flanks of an armoured thrust to protect it and, in addition to tank-killing, it has considerable anti-helicopter capability. Main anti-tank armament is four AT-2 Swatter or AT-3 Sagger missiles for Hind D, and four AT-6 Spirals for Hind E. Extensive sensor and electronic countermeasures (ECM) suites are carried, and a variety of guns, the largest of which is the 23mm GSh-23L.

First flight: c.1971. Operational c.1974. **Users:** Afghanistan, Algeria, Bulgaria, Czechoslovakia, East Germany, Hungary, Iraq, Poland, South Yemen, USSR.

Below: The Hind D is really a battlefield support helicopter rather than a dedicated tank-killer in the Western style.

TANK BUSTERS

Mil Mi-28 Havoc

The new Soviet attack helicopter (given the reporting name Havoc by NATO) had not been seen by Western eyes by early 1987, and it is believed that all information released so far is a product of satellite photography, and it is thus conjectural.

From the data so far available, it appears that Havoc has adopted the two-seat tandem crew position and narrow fuselage cross-section séen in many Western types, with the engines widely separated on the upper sides. A five-bladed rotor is driven by what probably are the same engines used by Hind, although it seems probable that the rotor head has been improved to aid manoeuvrability.

Havoc is smaller and lighter than Hind, although rather larger and con-

AIRCRAFT

siderably heavier than Apache, while disc loading is appreciably less than that of either, which should make for good climb and acceleration.

The main anti-tank weapons are eight AT-6 Spirals mounted beneath the stub wings, and the usual alternatives can be carried as well as air-to-air missiles. What appears to be a new design of 30mm gun is mounted beneath the nose. The avionics fit is likely to be comprehensive, and a radome is shown on the nose.

A further helicopter from the Kamov stable codenamed Hokum is also under development; this is in the HueyCobra weight range, and is depicted as having twin co-axial contra-rotating rotors with aircraft-style tail surfaces.

First flight (Havoc): c.1982. Operational with USSR c.1988.

Below: An artist's impression of the Mil Mi-28 Havoc, which is expected to carry AT-6 missiles and a new 30mm cannon.

TANK BUSTERS

Westland Lynx AH-1

The Lynx was designed as a multi-purpose tactical helicopter, but the plethora of roles that it can perform have not prejudiced its effectiveness as a tank-killer. In many ways it is ideal, with unsurpassed agility, instant response to control inputs, and virtually no flight envelope restrictions. The demonstrated roll rate exceeds 100 degrees per second, and it can turn hard enough to pull the rotor clean out of a Hind should it be unwise enough to try and follow.

Entirely of Westland design, 30 per cent of the construction was shared with Aérospatiale, on the assumption that France would buy an equal proportion of the production, which has not proved to be the case. Despite this, the Lynx has sold to 10 nations to date against world competition. The multi-role requirement virtually dictated the use of side-by-side seating for the pilot and gunner in order to accommodate a cabin behind them. Ten fully armed troops can be carried (not in much comfort, it must be admitted), or three stretcher cases plus an attendant. A more aggressive alternative is three gunners with their anti-tank launchers and missiles.

The main anti-tank weapons are eight TOW missiles carried four on each side on outriggers and, to prolong combat persistence, a further eight reloads can be

AIRCRAFT

carried in the cabin, for a total of 16 on-board kills — higher than anything bar the Apache. HOT is an alternative primary load, as is Hellfire. Lynx is also cleared to carry the DAT mine dispenser (for laying a minefield in the path of an armoured advance). A wide mix of secondary weapons, unguided rockets and so on can be carried. Cannon are optional, and are often not fitted. Missile aiming is via a roof-mounted sight.

The four-bladed rotor is powered by two Rolls Royce Gem 2 turboshafts, which give Lynx an excellent top speed and rate of climb. Construction is conventional, as one would expect of a design over 15 years old, but it is very sturdy, and gave sterling service in the Falklands War of 1982.

Westland proposed an uprated Lynx AH-3 in the early 1980s for British Army Air Corps use. This would have been slightly larger and more powerful, making use of advanced composites. Main armament was to have been either eight or 16 Hellfire missiles, plus Stingers for air defence. This was dropped in favour of the Mangusta.

First flight: 21 March 1971. **Users:** Argentina, Belgium, Brazil, Denmark, France, Holland, Norway, Qatar, UK, West Germany.

Below: The Lynx, shown here with roof-mounted sight and TOW missiles, is both fast and extremely agile.

Missiles, Rockets, Air-launched Scatter Weapons

THE MAIN battle tank has been considered the primary offensive land weapon for so many years that it is hardly surprising that a considerable amount of ingenuity and effort has been devoted to developing weapons to stop it. These range from the barely credible to the barely affordable, and the sheer variety is bewildering. Often there is an overlap in their method of usage; some weapons are man-portable but can also be carried on vehicles and helicopters. It can also be difficult to draw the line between an air-launched guided missile and a powered smart bomb, or a cluster bomb and a stand-off dispenser, while in other cases a cluster bomb can form the base of a smart bomb.

Where the same weapon has both an air- and ground-launched application, it has been mentioned under the heading of its primary use. There are other weapons not included in this section which also overlap with the general heading; notable among these are the smart shells and dispensing munitions, often carried by rocket, which have been dealt with as artillery. Mines can also be laid in this manner.

Ground-launched Guided Missiles

A tremendous variety of ground-launched guided missiles are currently in service, the vast majority of which use a command to line of sight (CLOS) system with wires to relay the manoeuvre commands from the operator to the missile. In most cases the system is semi-automatic, the operator needing only to keep the cross-hairs in the sight centred on the target while the guidance system tracks the missile (which carries a flare, usually IR, although a tungsten lamp is carried by the American M47 Dragon, and xenon lamps by the Japanese KAM-9) and the black boxes signal compensatory commands to keep the missile on target. Two missiles using alternative systems are the Soviet AT-8 and the Israeli MAPATS, which use laser beam riding.

Manoeuvre is commonly by aerodynamic surfaces which 'flip-out' after launch, although jet deflection is used by some, such as the venerable AT-3 Sagger and the British Swingfire, while MILAN uses thrust vectoring. Which method is used is a matter of choice at the design stage; only at the extreme limit of range does it become crucial. With thrust vectoring or jet deflection, control is obviously lost when the sustainer motor burns out, whereas aerodynamic surfaces give

Fibre-optic control for tactical missiles

Wire-guided AT missiles are widely used where there is a clear line-of-sight between controller and target. But fibre-optics offer the possibility of firing and controlling weapons from safety behind obstacles. A video camera in the missile's nose passes real-time pictures to the controller, who directs the missile down onto the target. Such systems could be secure, cheap, and hard to counter.

The opportunity to knock out an MBT costing millions of dollars with a cheap weapon costing tens of thousands seems at first a real bargain — but, if things were really that simple, tanks would long ago have been consigned to museums. The fact is that a continuing battle is being waged between the tank designer and the missile and weapon designer, first one having the advantage, then the other. The current situation is confused, with claims and counter-claims being made by both parties. The West is backing missiles; the Soviets seem to be sold on reactive armour.

control until speed decays.

The propulsion unit usually functions in two stages: launch, which propels the missile from the launcher at a relatively low speed, and is all-burnt by the time the missile leaves the launcher, thus protecting the crewman from exhaust burns; then, after a preset distance, the sustainer motor accelerates the missile to its design speed before burning out. The most extreme example of this is the French Eryx, which launches at a mere 66ft/s (20m/s) before accelerating to a maximum of 984ft/s (300m/s). Speeds vary between the 280ft/s (85m/s) of the German Cobra 2000 and the 1,083ft/s (330m/s) of the American TOW II. These speeds translate to 191mph (306km/h), and 738mph (1,188km/h) respectively, TOW II travelling at Mach 0.97.

Far more important from the operator's point of view is the time of flight: how long the missile takes to impact the target, which is also how long the operator, who may well be cold, tired, wet, and not a little perturbed, has to hold the sight on target. M47 Dragon, which is one of the shorter-ranged weapons, takes a full 11 seconds to reach out a mere 3,280ft (1,000m), while TOW I takes only 15 seconds to achieve three times this distance.

Maximum effective range is also important; the operator will always prefer to engage targets as far away as visibility, terrain, and the weapon permits. Eryx, which is one of the most modern weapons listed, has an effective range of only 1,970ft (600m), while other modern weapons such as AT-6 Kobra, Swingfire, and HOT, have a reach of 13,120ft (4,000m), and most of the others can exceed 6,560ft (2,000m).

At the other extreme, there is an effective minimum range, which is set by a combination of factors such as the launch speed, the time taken for the missile to arm, and the time the guidance system takes to gather the missile under control. This varies from Eryx and MILAN, with 82ft (25m), to the 1,970ft (600m) of the antiquated AT-2 Swatter, with an ▶

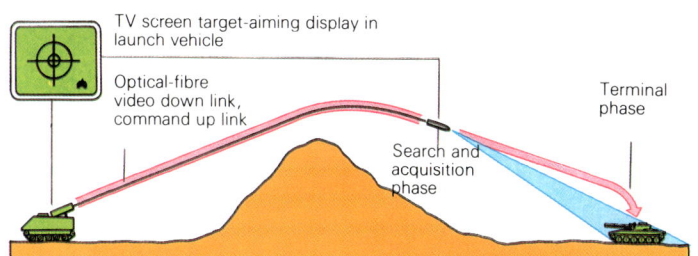

TANK BUSTERS

▶ average of around 200ft (60m) for the modern missiles. This, it should be stated, is for a static target; the distance sometimes as much as doubles for a moving target.

Warheads are, without exception, of the hollow-charge (HC) type, and vary between the 100mm diameter of the Cobra 2000 and the 170mm of the AT-5 Spandrel. Armour penetration is a vexed subject, made even more complex by the development of composite armour and improved warhead design. Manufacturers' claims for the more modern missiles range between 31.5 and 51.2 in (800 and 1,300mm) penetration of homogenous rolled-steel armour, while Swingfire is claimed to be able to defeat all known armour combinations. If it were this simple, the scrapyards would be full of discarded tanks.

That it is not is simply demonstrated by the interest being shown in a Bofors product, the RBS 56 BILL. This appears to be a run-of-the-mill SACLOS guided medium-range anti-tank missile, but it has one very interesting feature. The line of

Ground-launched Guided Missiles

Name	Origin	Platform	Guidance	Control link	Control	Calibre in(mm)	Length ft(m)
AT-2 Swatter	USSR	port/veh/helo	MCLOS	radio	aerodynamic	5.2 (132)	3.71 (1.13)
AT-3 Sagger	USSR	port/veh/helo	MCLOS	wire	jet deflect.	4.7 (119)	2.82 (0.86)
AT-4 Spigot	USSR	man-portable	SACLOS	wire	aerodynamic	5.1 (130)	3.61 (1.10)
AT-5 Spandrel	USSR	vehicle	SACLOS	wire	aerodynamic	6.7 (170)	4.27 (1.30)
AT-8 Kobra	USSR	tank gun	SA laser	beam rider	aerodynamic	4.92 (125)	n/a
BGM-71A TOW I	USA	port/veh/helo	SACLOS	wire	aerodynamic	6 (152)	3.84 (1.17)
BGM-71B TOW II	USA	port/veh/helo	SACLOS	wire	aerodynamic	6 (152)	4.59 (1.40)
Cobra 2000	W. Germany	man portable	MCLOS	wire	aerodynamic	4 (100)	3.12 (0.95)
Eryx	France	man portable	SACLOS	wire	aerodynamic	6.30 (160)	2.97 (0.905)
HOT 1	France/Germany	veh/helo	SACLOS	wire	jet deflect.	6.5 (165)	4.17 (1.27)
HOT 2	France/Germany	veh/helo	SACLOS	wire	jet deflect.	6.5 (165)	4.17 (1.27)
KAM-3D	Japan	port/veh/helo	MCLOS	wire	aerodynamic	4.72 (120)	3.33 (1.015)
KAM-9	Japan	vehicle	SACLOS	wire	aerodynamic	6 (152)	5.13 (1.565)
Kuen Wu	Taiwan	vehicle	MCLOS	wire	jet deflect.	4.69 (119)	2.89 (0.88)
M47 Dragon	USA	man portable (disp.)	SACLOS	wire	jet deflect.	5 (127)	2.44 (0.744)

MISSILES, ROCKETS, SCATTER WEAPONS

sight followed by the missile is about 3ft (1m) above the operator's line of sight, and it has a hollow-charge warhead angled down at 30 degrees. As it is about to overfly the target, the warhead is detonated downwards to attack the thin top armour of the tank.

Ground-launched Unguided Missiles

An infantry weapon has to be light, cheap, and easy to use. As its effective range is short, it should not betray the operator's position when launched, or he will become vulnerable to counter-attack. Ideally it should be usable from a confined position, such as inside a building, although this requirement is not often met.

The effectiveness of a hollow-charge warhead is to a great degree linked to its diameter. But the larger the diameter, the greater the weight, not only of the projectile but of the propellant, and also the launcher. The launcher consists of a more or less simple tube, with a sighting ▶

Weight lb(kg)	Warhead	Launch speed ft/s (m/s)	Flight speed ft/s (m/s)	Flt duration ft(m) — secs	Min. range ft(m)	Max.range ft(m)	Penetration in(mm)
25 (11.3)	HC	n/a	490 (150)	n/a	1,970 (600)	8,200 (2,500)	15.75 (400+)
24 (11)	HC 6lb (2.7kg)	n/a	390 (120)	9,843 (3,000) 25 secs	1,640 (500)	9,843 (3,000)	15.75 (400+)
26 (12)	HEAT	590 (180)	490 (150)	6,562 (2,000) 11 secs	n/a	6,560 (2,000)	19.68 (500+)
40 (18)	HEAT	n/a	656 (200)	n/a	n/a	13,100 (4,000)	19.68 (500+)
n/a	HEAT	n/a	n/a	n/a	n/a	13,124 (4,000)	n/a
42 (18.90)	HC 127mm dia.	n/a	1,024 (312)	9,840 (3,000) 15 secs	213 (65)	12,300 (3,750)	n/a
47 (21.50)	HC 150mm dia.	n/a	1,083 (330)	n/a	213 (65)	12,300 (3,750)	n/a
23 (10.30)	HC 100mm dia.	n/a	280 (85)	n/a	1,312 (400)	6,560 (2,000)	19.68 (500)
24 (11)	HC 135mm dia.	66 (20)	984 (300)	1,970 (600) 4 secs	82 (25)	1,970 (600)	35.43 (900)
52 (23.50)	HC, 6.6lb (3kg) HE	n/a	820 (250)	9,843 (3,000) 13 secs	246 (75)	13,124 (4,000)	31.5 (900+)
52 (23.50)	HC, 9lb (4.1kg) HE	n/a	820 (250)	9,843 (3,000) 13 secs	246 (75)	13,124 (4,000)	51.2 (1,300+)
35 (15.70)	HC	n/a	280 (85)	n/a	1,150 (350)	5,900 (1,800)	n/a
73 (33)	HC, 17lb (7.5kg)	n/a	656 (200)	13,124 (4,000) 20 secs	n/a	13,124 (4,000)	19.7 (500+)
25 (11.3)	HC, 6lb (2.7kg) HE	n/a	394 (120)	n/a	1,640 (500)	9,843 (3,000)	19.7 (500)
13.6 (6.17)	HC, 5.4lb (2.44kg) HE	n/a	328 (100)	3,280 (1,000) 11 secs	197 (60)	3,280 (1,000)	23.6 (600)

Table continued on next page

TANK BUSTERS

Table continued from previous page

Name	Origin	Platform	Guidance	Control link	Control	Calibre in(mm)	Length ft(m)
Mamba	W Germany	man-portable	CLOS	wire	aerodynamic	4.72 (120)	3.13 (0.955)
MAPATS	Israel	port/veh	laser	laser beam rider	aerodynamic	5.83/(148)	4.76 (1.45)
Mathogo	Argentina	veh/helo	MCLOS	wire	aerodynamic	4 (102)	3.27 (0.998)
MILAN 2	France	man portable	SACLOS	wire	vectored thrust	4.57 (116)	2.53 (0.77)
RBS56 BILL	Sweden	port/veh	SACLOS	wire	aerodynamic	5.9 (150)	2.95 (0.90)
Red Arrow	PR of China	man portable	MCLOS	wire	vector nozzles	4.72 (120)	2.85 (0.868)
Red Arrow 8	PR of China	man portable	SACLOS	wire	jet deflect.	4.72 (120)	2.87 (0.875)
Swingfire	UK	vehicle	MCLOS	wire	jet deflect.	6.69 (170)	3.48 (1.06)

*Penetration figures are for homogenous armour.

Folgore infantry anti-tank weapon

Typical of the latest infantry AT weapons is the Breda 80mm Folgore, a recoilless cannon with a maximum effective range (using the tripod and rangefinder) of 3,280 ft (1,000m). The diagrams on the right show the flight trajectories and times of the Folgore. The missile speed is crucial: the Folgore can reach a target at 3,280ft in 3 seconds, during which time a tank, travelling at 30mph (48km/h) could have moved 132ft (40.25m).

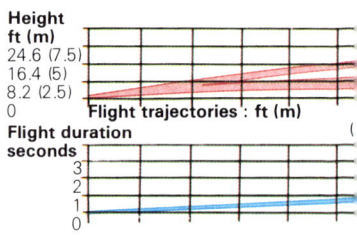

Air-launched Guided Missiles

Name	Origin	Platform	Calibre in(mm)	Length ft(m)	Launch wt lb(kg)	Target acquisition
AGM-65A Maverick	USA	fixed wing	12 (305)	8.16 (2.49)	462 (210)	EO
AGM-65B Maverick	USA	fixed wing	12 (305)	8.16 (2.49)	462 (210)	EO
AGM-65D Maverick	USA	fixed wing	12 (305)	8.16 (2.49)	485 (220)	IIR
AS30 Laser	France	fixed wing	13.46 (342)	11.98 (3.65)	1,146 (520)	SA laser
AGM-114A Hellfire	USA	helo	7 (177.8)	5.33 (1.626)	99 (45)	laser desig.
AT-6 Spiral	USSR	fixed wing, helo	5.5 (140)	5.90 (1.80)	n/a	optical?
HVM	USA	fixed wing, helo	3.8 (96.5)	n/a	48.5 (22)	MICOS (laser radar)

MISSILES, ROCKETS, SCATTER WEAPONS

Weight lb(kg)	Warhead	Launch speed ft/s (m/s)	Flight speed ft/s (m/s)	Flt duration ft(m) — secs	Min. range ft(m)	Max. range ft(m)	Penetration in(m)*
24 (11)	HC, 6lb (2.7kg) HE	180 (55)	459 (140)	3,280 (1,000) 10 secs	984 (300)	6,560 (2,000)	18.7 (450)
41 (18.5)	HC, 7.9lb (3.6kg) HE	230 (70)	1,033 (315)	13,120 (4,000) 19.5 secs	n/a	13,125 (4,000)	31.5 (800)
25 (11.3)	HC 102mm dia.	n/a	295 (90)	n/a	1,148 (350)	6,900 (2,100)	n/a
15 (6.7)	HC 115mm dia.	246 (75)	656 (200)	6,560 (2,000) 12.5 secs	82 (25)	6,560 (2,000)	39.4 (1000)
9.25 (4.2)	HC 30° angled	n/a	656 (200)	6562 (2000) 10 secs	492 (150)	6,562 (2,000)	n/a (top attack)
25 (11.3)	HEAT	n/a	394 (120)	n/a	1,640 (500)	3,280 (1,000)	17.7 (450)
24.7 (11.2)	HC 120mm dia.	n/a	787 (240)	n/a	328 (100)	9,840 (3,000)	31.5 (800)
62 (28)	HC 15.4lb (7kg) HE	n/a	607 (185)	13,125 (4,000) 26 secs	492 (150)	13,125 (4,000)	all known armour

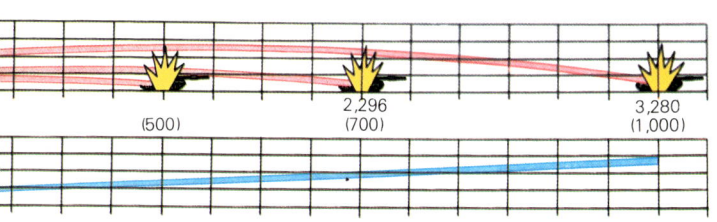

(500)   2,296 (700)   3,280 (1,000)

Homing	Control	Velocity	Min. range ft(m)	Max. range ft(m)	Warhead	Penetration
EO contrast	aerodynamic	subsonic	3,200 (1,000)	52,000 (16,000)	HC, 125lb (57kg)	all known armour
EO contrast	aerodynamic	subsonic	3,200 (1,000)	52,000 (16,000)	HC, 125lb (57kg)	all known armour
IIIR contrast	aerodynamic	subsonic	3,200 (1,000)	52,000 (16,000)	HC, 125lb (57kg)	all known armour
laser desig.	aerodynamic	supersonic	n/a	37,000 (11,250)	HE or SAP 529lb (240kg)	all known armour
SA laser	aerodynamic	888mph (1,430km/h)	n/a	19,700 (6,000)	HC, 20lb (9kg)	27.5in (700mm)
radio command	aerodynamic	622mph (1,000km/h)	1,650 (500)	16,400 (5,000)	HEAT 18–22lb (8–10kg)	25.6in (650mm+)
CO_2 laser beam riding	thrust squibs	5,000ft/s (1,500m/s)	n/a	6,000 (1,800)	KEP	n/a

TANK BUSTERS

Ground-launched Unguided Missiles

Name	Origin	Launcher details			Disposable	Crew number	Restrictions
		Length ft(m)	Calibre in(mm)	Weight lb(kg)			
AC300 Jupiter	France/W. Germany	3.94 (1.20)	2.75 (70)	17 (7.6)	Yes	1	none
ACL-STRIM	France	5.25 (1.60)	3.5 (88.9)	19 (8.6)	no	1	confined space
Apilas	France	4.27 (1.30)	4.41 (112)	10 (4.7)	yes	1	confined space
Armbrust	W.Germany	2.79 (0.85)	2.95 (75)	19 (8.5)	yes	1	confined space
B300	Israel	4.43 (1.35)	3.23 (82)	8 (3.5)	semi	1	n/a
C-90C & D	Spain	3.08 (0.94)	3.54 (90)	9 (3.9)	yes	1	confined space
Carl Gustav M2-550	Sweden	3.70 (1.13)	3.31 (84)	33 (15)	no	1	confined space
Folgore	Italy	6.07 (1.85)	3.15 (80)	60 (27)	no	1 or 2	n/a
LAW 80	UK	4.92 (1.50)	3.70 (94)	21 (9.6)	yes	1	confined space
64mm LAW	Yugoslavia	n/a	2.5 (64)	n/a	n/a	1	n/a
M57 launcher	Yugoslavia	n/a	1.73 (44)	18 (8.2)	no	2	confined space
M65 launcher	Spain	5.38 (1.64)	3.5 (88.9)	13 (6)	no	1	confined space
M72A2 & A3	USA	2.93 (0.89)	2.60 (66)	3 (1.36)	yes	1	n/a
M72 750 LAW	USA	3.09 (0.94)	2.6 (66)	7 (3)	yes	1	n/a
Panzerfaust 3	W.Germany	3.94 (1.20)	2.36 (60)	26 (12)	no	2	none
Pzf44 2A1 Lanze	W.Germany	3.81 (1.16)	1.73 (44)	17 (7.8)	no	1	none
62mm portable launcher	PR of China	n/a	2.44 (62)	n/a	yes	1	n/a
RBRM 80	Yugoslavia	n/a	2.5 (64)	n/a	no	2	confined space
RLC-83	Belgium	3.94 (1.20)	3.27 (83)	14 (6.2)	no	2	confined space
RPG-7	USSR	3.25 (0.99)	1.57 (40)	15 (7)	no	1	confined space
RPG-18	USSR	n/a	2.52 (64)	9 (4)	no	1	confined space
RPG-75	Czechoslovakia	2.92 (0.89)	2.68 (68)	7 (3.1)	yes	1	confined space
Sabracan	France	n/a	5.12 (130)	29 (13)	semi	n/a	none

MISSILES, ROCKETS, SCATTER WEAPONS

Missile details

Length ft(m)	Calibre in(mm)	Weight lb(kg)	Warhead	Launch speed ft/s(m/s)	Max. speed ft/s(m/s)	Effective AT range ft(m)	Flight duration ft(m)-secs	Penetration in(mm)
n/a	4.5 (115)	8 (3.5)	HC 115mm dia.	590 (180)	902 275	984 (300)	n/a	31.5 (800+)
1.97 (0.60)	3.5 (88.9)	5 (2.2)	HC 80mm dia.	955 (291)	n/a	1,312 (400)	1,312 (400) 1.46 secs	18.9 (480)
3.03 (0.93)	4.4 (112)	9.5 (4.3)	HC 112mm dia.	961 (293)	n/a	984 (300)	1,640 (500) 1.9 secs	27.5 (700+)
n/a	4.5 (115)	8 (3.5)	HEAT	689 (210)	n/a	984 (300)	984 (300) 1.5 secs	31.5 (800+)
n/a	3.23 (82)	7 (3)	HEAT	920 (280)	n/a	1,312 (400)	n/a	15.75 (400)
n/a	3.54 (90)	5 (2.35)	HC	607 (185)	n/a	984 (300)	n/a	17.7 (450)
n/a	3.31 (84)	5 (2.2)	HEAT	853 (260)	1,148 (350)	2,300 (700)	2,300 (700) 2.2 secs	15.75 (400)
2.43 (0.74)	3.15 (80)	11 (5.2)	HC	1,247 (380)	1,640 (500)	3,280 (1,000)	n/a	n/a
n/a	3.70 (94)	n/a	HC 90mm dia.	n/a	n/a	1,640 (500)	n/a	23.6 (600+)
n/a	2.5 (64)	n/a	HEAT	n/a	n/a	820 (250)	n/a	11.8 (300)
n/a	Over-calibre	5 (2.4)	HEAT	n/a	n/a	656 (200)	n/a	11.8 (300)
n/a	3.5 (88.9)	5 (2.3)	HEAT	705 (215)	n/a	1,476 (450)	n/a	16.9 (430)
1.67 (0.51)	2.60 (66)	2 (1)	HC, 340g HE	475 (145)	n/a	984 (300)	n/a	12 (305)
n/a	2.6 (66)	n/a	HC	n/a	n/a	1,640 (500)	820 (250) 1.2 secs	15 (380)
n/a	4.33/(110)	8 (3.8)	HC 110mm dia.	558 (170)	820 (250)	1,640 (500)	984 (300) 1.3 secs	27.5 (700+)
1.80 (0.55)	2.64 (67)	3 (1.5)	HC 67mm dia.	551 (168)	689 (210)	1,312 (400)	n/a	14.5 (370+)
1.78 (0.54)	2.44 (62)	2.6 (1.18)	HEAT	n/a	n/a	492 (150)	n/a	4 (100)
n/a	3.94 (100)	n/a	HEAT	n/a	n/a	n/a	n/a	n/a
2.20 (0.67)	3.5 (89)	6 (2.7)	HEAT	328 (100)	984 (300)	1,476 (450)	1,640 (500) 1.95 secs	10.8 (275)
n/a	3.35 (85)	5 (2.25)	HEAT	984 (300)	n/a	1,640 (500)	n/a	12.6 (320)
n/a	Over-calibre	5.5 (2.5)	HEAT	374 (114)	n/a	656 (200)	n/a	11.8 (300)
n/a	Over-calibre	n/a	HC	620 (189)	n/a	984 (300)	n/a	n/a
n/a	5.12 (130)	10 (4.5)	HC 130mm dia.	n/a	n/a	1,970 (600)	n/a	31.5 (800+)

TANK BUSTERS

Air-launched Unguided Rockets

Name	Origin	Platform	Launcher & qty	Length ft(m)	Calibre in(mm)	Weight lb(kg)
135mm Bofors	Sweden	FW	pod, 6	n/a	5.3 (135)	99 (45)
2in BPD	Italy	FW/helo	pod,14, 18,25,28,29	3.44 (1.05)	2 (51)	10.5 (4.8)
81mm BPD	Italy	FW/helo	pod,6,7,12	5.15 (1.57)	3.19 (81)	35 (15.9)
122mm BPD	Italy	FW/helo	pod,3,4	8.20 (2.50)	4.80 (122)	132 (60)
CRV 7	Canada	FW/helo	tube,6,19	n/a	2.76 (70)	15.5 (7)
SBAT-70	Brazil	FW/helo	pod,7,19	n/a	2.76 (70)	n/a
SNORA 81 RAK 026/054	Switzerland	FW/helo	multi-rails,12	4.95 (1.51)	3.19 (81)	26(12)
SURA-D	Switzerland	FW/helo	multi-rails,12	3.98 (1.21)	3.19 (81)	26 (12)
TBA 68 253ECC	France	FW/helo	pod,12,22	2.99 (0.91)	2.68 (68)	11 (5)
TBA 100 ECC	France	FW/helo	pod,4	8.20 (2.50)	3.94 (100)	84 (38)
TBA 100 AB24 multi-projectiles	France	FW	pod,12,22	8.99 (2.74)	3.94 (100)	89 (40.5)

▶ system of greater or lesser complexity, and a firing mechanism, which can be electromagnetic, percussion, or mechanical. Some weapons have a bipod, which aids accurate firing at longer ranges, but which adds to the carry weight.

The launch tube is often made telescopic for ease of carrying, and a growing trend has appeared to make it disposable after the round has been fired. If the sighting system is telescopic, or has a night-sight facility, this can generally be detached and is retained, or in at least one case is fitted to the next launch tube, which comes prepacked with projectile. In some cases the firing mechanism is also re-usable in the same way.

Apart from the quality of the sighting system, accuracy depends on two things: the ratio of length of launcher to calibre, and the ballistic qualities of the projectile. The ballistics are beyond the scope of this work, but the length-calibre relationship can be summarised. At its simplest, the longer the launcher, the more accurate the shooting, but this also adds to weight and to cost. The infantry anti-tank weapon tends to be a compromise, with error increasing in proportion to cheapness.

Air-launched Guided Missiles

This subsection covers those missiles specifically designed to be air-launched, rather than types like TOW, which have multiple applications. Their development arose from a need to give aircraft, either fixed-wing or helicopters, improved survivability over the battlefield together with a vastly enhanced kill probability. Survivability is achieved by reducing the aircraft exposure time, which is done by increasing the range at which the target is engaged and using launch-and-leave missiles.

As a general rule, the air-launched anti-tank missile is larger, more complex, and far more expensive than its ground-launched counterpart. It carries a warhead large enough virtually to assure the destruction of any tank hit, and it is very reliable.

The most widely used Western missile in this category is the AGM-65 Maverick in its various forms, which uses either electro-

MISSILES, ROCKETS, SCATTER WEAPONS

Warhead	Motor burn time secs	Launch speed ft/s (m/s)	Min. range ft(m)	Max. range ft(m)	Flight duration ft(m)-secs	Penetration in(mm)
AP,5kg HE	2	1,970 (600)	n/a	6,56 (2,000)	6.56 3.5 secs	n/a
AT-AP	1.1	1,690 (515)	n/a	n/a	n/a	n/a
AT-AP	0.85	2,067 (630)	n/a	n/a	n/a	n/a
HEAT	1.21	2,460 (750)	n/a	n/a	n/a	n/a
KEP	n/a	4,100 (1,250)	3,280 (1,000)	21,325 (6,500)	n/a	n/a
AVC-70 HEAT	1.2	n/a	n/a	n/a	n/a	n/a
HC, 1kgHE	n/a	2,690 (820)	n/a	32,810 (10,000)	6,562 (2,000) 3.2 secs	13.75 (350+)
HC	0.9	1,950 (595)	n/a	6,562 (2,000)	n/a	n/a
HC	n/a	1,970 (600)	3,280 (1,000)	13,125 (4,000)	n/a	15.75 (400)
HC 100mm dia.	n/a	2,495 (760)	3,280 (1,000)	13,125 (4,000)	13,125 (4,000) 6 secs	19.68 (500)
6x24mm dia. darts	n/a	1,640 (500) (impact velocity)	3,280 (1,000)	13,125 (4,000)	n/a	3.15 (80)

optical (EO) or imaging infra-red (IIR) active guidance, flies at high sub-sonic speeds, and uses aerodynamic control surfaces. It is essentially a fixed-wing aircraft weapon. AGM-114A Hellfire is its rotary-wing counterpart, using SA laser guidance, while the Soviet Union fields the AT-6 Spiral, which is believed to use IR tracking together with radio command guidance.

Currently under development in this category is the LTV Hyper-Velocity Missile (HVM). This is totally different to the others in this category, as it is small, cheap, and uses high speed coupled with a kinetic energy penetrator (KEP) to destroy its target. With a launch weight of just 48.5lb (22kg), it flies at 5,000ft/s (1,520m/s), roughly Mach 4.5. Guidance is by carbon dioxide laser, and control by a ring of 'squib' thrusters around the nose coupled with roll stabilisation.

With a very short time of flight, approximately 1.5 seconds, little control adjustment will be needed; the period that the launch aircraft spends in target designation is minimised, while the target stands little chance of taking successful evasive action, even if aware of the attack. Finally, the light weight and low cost of the HVM means that many of them can be carried. HVM may well become the fixed-wing aircraft anti-tank weapon of the future.

Air-launched Unguided Rockets

The unguided rocket has never really lost favour as an anti-tank weapon, and modern design has improved the range, accuracy, and lethality, although it is still in the main used as a shotgun-type weapon. It is carried by both fixed-wing aircraft and helicopters, and there are disadvantages in both cases. The operational range of these weapons, which is generally limited by the distance at which a target can be acquired, is fairly short, so that a fast jet is committed to overflying the defences. On the other hand, the helicopter does not have the forward speed necessary to increase the velocity of the rockets.

A tremendous range of unguided rockets is available; the table lists ▶

TANK BUSTERS

only those most commonly used, or those of particular interest. Warheads are generally of the hollow-charge type, and calibres vary between 51mm and 135mm. (The Soviet Union fields some much larger types, but little firm information is available.) One basic rule of thumb is that the larger the calibre, the fewer the aircraft can carry, and the smaller the shotgun pattern, which in turn reduces the hit probability, while the smaller the calibre, the larger the hit probability, but the smaller the kill probability per hit.

Two recent developments that are of unusual interest are the Canadian CRV 7, and the French Multi-Projectile. CRV 7 is a high-velocity, very accurate weapon, generally launched in pairs. It uses a kinetic energy long rod penetrator, possibly of depleted uranium.

The French weapon uses the TBA 100 warhead which opens at a preset range to discharge a sheaf of flechettes at very high velocity. The carrier rocket is salvoed to give coverage to a large area. While the penetration capability of the flechette is not really sufficient to qualify it as a tank-killer, it is an interesting development and would be effective against light armour.

Rocket Launch Systems

There are almost as many rocket launch systems available as there are rockets. These are usually in pod

Rocket Launch Systems

Name	Origin	Platform	Configuration
Aerea AL-6-80	Italy	FW	pod
Aerea HL-7-80	Italy	helo	pod
Aerea SAL-12-80	Italy	supersonic FW	pod
Brandt 100-4(F3)	France	FW/helo	tube
CASA 18.070	Spain	FW/helo	pod
HYDRA 70(M261)	USA	helo	pod
LANCO RC-06-100	Spain	FW	rack
MATRA RL F1	France	FW/helo	pod
MATRA RL F4	France	FW/helo	pod
Oerlikon HL-7-80 (RWK 022)	Switzerland	helo	pod
Oerlikon SAL-6-80 (RWK-021)	Switzerland	supersonic FW	pod

form, but often in racks or rails. Some pods are small and light, and can be carried by a light aircraft or helicopter, while others are large, to give maximum firepower. Batteries of unguided rockets are often referred to as being salvoed, but the correct term is ripple fired. Differing rates of fire give varying spreads on the ground, and are used to meet differing operational needs. The variation in fire rate ranges from 6.66 per second for the Brandt 100-4 (F3), pod, to 50 per second for the Lanco rack. Taking an aircraft flying at 550mph (886km/h), this would give a theoretical spread between projectiles of 122ft (37m) in the first in-

Below: The Eryx missile, which has a low muzzle velocity. It can be used in an enclosed space.

MISSILES, ROCKETS, SCATTER WEAPONS

Length ft(m)	Diameter ft(mm)	Empty weight lb(kg)	Proj. calibre in(mm)	No. of rockets	Rate of fire
7.26 (2.21)	0.97 (296)	84 (38)	3.19 (81)	6	10/sec
5.91 (1.80)	0.97 (296)	73 (33)	3.19 (81)	7	10/sec
8.53 (2.60)	1.30 (396)	146 (66)	3.19 (81)	8	10/sec
9.51 (2.90)	0.755x0.79 (230x240)	154 (70)	3.94 (100)	4	6.66/sec
4.07 (1.24)	1.31 (40)	82 (36.4)	2.75 (70)	18	33/sec
5.42 (1.65)	1.33 (406)	82 (36.4)	2.75 (70)	19	16.67/sec
11.16 (3.40)	n/a	220 (100)	3.94 (100)	6	14–50/sec
6.98 (2.13)	1.85(565)	95 (43.2)	2.68 (68)	36	33.33/sec
7.69 (2.34)	1.35 (410)	158 (71.6)	2.68 (68)	18	33.33/sec
5.91 (1.80)	0.97 (296)	73 (33)	3.19 (81)	7	10/sec
8.53 (2.60)	0.97 (296)	106 (48)	3.19 (81)	7	10/sec

stance, and 16ft (5m) in the second.

Racks and tubes tend to create a lot of drag, which is undesirable on a fast jet, although of less importance on a rotary-wing craft. Pods, often constructed of fibreglass to keep the ▶

Smart Bombs

Name	Origin	Base bomb	Bomb weight lb(kg)	Guidance	Power	Range* miles (km)
AGM-123A Skipper	USA	Mk83	1,000 (450)	laser	rocket	n/a
AGM-130A**	USA	Mk84	2,000 (900)	EO or IIR	rocket	15 (24)
FAB 500 LGB	USSR	FAB 500	1,100 (500)	laser	none	3 (5)
FAB 750 LGB	USSR	FAB 750	1,650 (750)	laser	none	3(5)
FAB 1000 LGB	USSR	FAB 1000	2,200 (1,000)	laser	none	3(5)
GBU-10	USA	Mk84	2,000 (900)	Paveway II laser	none	3(5)
GBU-12	USA	Mk 82	500 (225)	Paveway II laser	none	3(5)
GBU-15 (V)**	USA	Mk84	2,000 (900)	EO	glide	5(8)
GBU-16	USA	Mk83	1,000 (450)	Paveway II laser	none	3 (5)
GBU-24	USA	Mk 84	2,000 (900)	Paveway III laser	glide	n/a
Mk 13/18	UK	n/a	1,000 (450)	Paveway II laser	none	3(5)
MATRA LGB	France	n/a	900 (400)	laser	none	3(5)
MATRA ARCOLE	France	n/a	2,200 (1,000)	laser	none	3(5)

*Approx. based on high-speed low-level delivery.
**Data-link command.

TANK BUSTERS

Air-launched Dispenser Weapons

Name	Origin	Loaded weight lb(kg)	Length ft(m)	Stand-off	Guidance	Range miles(km)
AALAAW	UK	n/a	n/a	glide	inertial/prog.	n/a
Alkan 530	France	298/(135)	n/a	captive	n/a	n/a
Apache CWS	France/W. Germany	2,200/(1,000)	13.12/(4.00)	glide	inertial	6.25/(10)
LAD	USA	3,000/(1,360)	n/a	glide	inertial/pre-prog.	5.5–12/(9–19)
MDS	W. Germany	3,858/(1,750)	variable	captive	n/a	n/a
CASMU disp.	Italy	2,315/(1,050)	15.61/(4.76)	glide	pre-prog.	3.6–7.5/(6–12)
Mobidic	France/W. Germany	n/a	n/a	rocket-powered	inertial	n/a
MW-1	W. Germany	n/a	17.39/(5.30)	captive	n/a	n/a
VBW	W. Germany	n/a	n/a	captive	n/a	n/a

Cluster Weapons

Name	Origin	Length ft(m)	Diameter ft(m)	Weight lb(kg)	Launch speed limit mph (km/h)	Launch height limit ft(m)
AVISPAS WB500F	Chile	8.17 (2.49)	1.45 (0.44)	500 (227)	609 (980)	n/a
Belouga	France	10.93 (3.33)	1.18 (0.36)	672 (305)	634 (1,020)	250 (75)
BL 755	UK	8.04 (2.45)	1.37 (0.42)	611 (277)	n/a	n/a
CB 130	Chile	6.73 (2.05)	0.83 (0.253)	132 (60)	653 (1,050)	n/a
CB 500	Chile	8.66 (2.64)	1.46 (0.446)	560 (254)	653 (1,050)	n/a
CB 1000	Chile	10.71 (3.27)	1.63 (0.49)	1,000 (454)	653 (1,050)	n/a
DPT-154	Yugoslavia	n/a	n/a	n/a	n/a	n/a
Expal BME 330	Spain	n/a	n/a	728 (330)	n/a	n/a
Rockeye II Mk 20	USA	7.87 (2.40)	1.10 (0.36)	489 (222)	n/a	250 (76)

MISSILES, ROCKETS, SCATTER WEAPONS

Launch speed limit mph(km/h)	Launch height limit ft(m)	Submunition details
n/a	n/a	Terminally guided submunitions
690/(1,110)	164/(50)	40 Brandt 74mm dia. HC grenades with AP capability of 8in (200mm+)
724/(1,163)	n/a	KB44 44mm HC bomblets, MIFF AT mines, Matra ACADIE or LASSO
n/a	n/a	n/a
684/(1,100)	164/(50)	n/a
n/a	n/a	n/a
n/a	n/a	n/a
n/a	n/a	4,536 KB44 44mm dia. HC bomblets or 872 MIFF 132mm dia. AT mines
n/a	250/(76)	AT HC grenades probably 80mm dia. – possibly same as used by LAW 80

Submunitions	Weight lb(kg)	Warhead	Penetration in(mm)
100	1.43 (0.65)	HC 53mm dia.	6 (150+)
151	2.86 (1.3)	HC 66mm dia.	n/a
147	n/a	HC 68mm dia.	10 (250+)
50	1.63 (0.74)	HC 48mm dia.	8 (203+)
240	63 (0.74)	HC 48mm dia.	8 (203+)
450	1.63 (0.74)	HC 48mm dia.	8 (203+)
44 PTAB	5.5 (2.5)	HC	n/a
180	n/a	HC	n/a
247	1.34 (0.61)	HC	n/a

▶ weight low, are in many ways a better solution. They carry a payload varying between six and 36 rockets in a low-drag housing.

Three basic types of pod exist: those for helicopter use, which tend to be flat-ended, and in which minimising weight is more important than lowering drag; those for fixed-wing aircraft use, which are pointed-nosed to reduce drag in exchange for a small weight penalty; and those that are compatible with supersonic aircraft, in which the nose is faired over with a light and frangible substance to minimise drag, and which protects the missiles from aerodynamic heating. This is for supersonic carriage only; so far as is known, no rockets are cleared for launch at supersonic speeds.

Smart Bombs

Quite a small bomb is capable of destroying an MBT; the clever bit is in hitting it. The nearest of near misses will rarely avail; the MBT is almost completely impervious to blast and splinters. To be effective against a tank-sized target, a far greater degree of accuracy is needed than is attainable with a free-fall 'iron' bomb.

The answer came with the development of a kit to convert old-fashioned iron bombs to guided 'smart' bombs. This was much cheaper than designing a guided weapon from scratch, and it also made stocks of existing bombs far more effective. The kit consisted of a laser homer in the nose, and larger tail fins. Since the mid 1960s, many nations have produced their own laser-guided bombs (LGBs).

Laser guidance is a form of passive homing. Laser light is reflected from a target, which is designated (or illuminated might be a better expression) from another source, either from another aeroplane or perhaps from the ground. The reflected laser light forms a basket above the target which pulls the LGB down into it with a fair degree of accuracy. However, the bomb must be released on a compatible speed and trajectory to work as advertised; if it is released in such a manner as to make it fall short, no amount of homing gear will stretch its flight; while if the ▶

TANK BUSTERS

Above: An A-10A Thunderbolt II test-fires one of its AGM-65 Maverick AT missiles.

▶ target is designated too early, the guidance unit acquires the target and starts pulling the bomb towards it too soon.

LGBs can either be released from medium altitudes at a long stand-off range, or they can be released from low altitude at an upward angle to lob into the target area. A range of roughly 3 miles (5km) can be achieved by this means.

Not all smart bombs use laser guidance; the Rockwell GBU-15(V) uses a television camera in the nose to relay what it can see back to the aircraft, from which it is guided by data link. Various means have been employed to increase the stand-off range of smart bombs; these include wings, with which they become glide bombs, while developments are currently afoot to fit rocket motors, which will extend the range considerably.

Smart bombs, as opposed to guided missiles, are generally although not always based on an existing iron bomb. Alternative base bombs are CBUs, or fuel-air bombs.

Cluster Weapons

The cluster bomb unit, or CBU, was originally developed as an area attack weapon. The effectiveness of small hollow-charge submunitions against thin armour gave the CBU an anti-tank capability as, falling vertically from above, the submunitions could attack the thin top armour.

Modern CBUs are designed to be released from low altitudes at high subsonic speeds. At a preset interval after release, the submunitions are ejected from the CBU casing, with differential ejection forces to give even scatter. With most models, the submunitions are armed shortly after ejection, and are slowed either by parachute or by retarding fins in order to achieve as near vertical impact angle on the target as possible. The hollow charge is detonated on impact.

As with most other simple weapons, a great many are in production, and the number of submunitions carried in each varies from less than 50 to many hundreds. Precise aiming is not needed; the scatter effect is designed to cover large areas with a fairly dense pattern, to maximise the hit probability. Most aircraft can carry many of these weapons, which can be released in quick succession. Many of them can also be fitted with a laser guidance kit to give them a stand-off capability.

Dispenser Weapons

Since a fast jet uses a combination of high speed and low altitude to survive over the battlefield, it gives itself some almost insoluble aiming problems against targets of opportunity. A solution that seems to be becoming rapidly accepted is the use of a dispenser to scatter submunitions over a wide area, using the same

MISSILES, ROCKETS, SCATTER WEAPONS

shotgun principle as the cluster weapon. At present, only two are in service: the French Alkan 530 which holds 40 74mm diameter Brandt hollow-charge grenades, and the much larger German Mehrzweckwaffe Eins, or MW-1, designed to be carried by Luftwaffe Tornados. Both of these dispensers are captive, and involve the aircraft overflying the target.

Also captive, and a very interesting variation on the theme, is the West German VBW, originally known as Vebal Syndrom. This is a small dispenser intended to be carried by the Alpha Jet. The submunitions are powered, and are individually launched downwards at an angle as the aircraft overflies a target array, launch being automatically triggered by sensors which select the warhead best placed to score a hit.

The overflight of target arrays in the modern battlefield is not the safest of occupations, and several stand-off dispensers are under development. The furthest advanced of these are glide weapons, with flip-out wings, such as the American Low-Altitude Dispenser (LAD), which has a range of up to 12 miles (19km). Navigation is by a combination of pre-programmed and inertial kit, while the submunitions are dispensed either on pre-programmed command or by on-board sensors. Further in the future is the British Advanced Air-Launched Anti-Armour Weapon (AALAAW), which has terminally guided submunitions.

The obvious next step, which is also under development, is the powered dispenser, which increases the stand-off distance. The Franco-German Apache/CWS is initially to be developed as a rocket-powered weapon, with later models being unpowered glide types, and later still a small turbojet will be fitted. This last may increase the cost of what is essentially a simple and cheap weapon system to the point where, unless terminally homing submunitions are carried, it becomes non cost-effective.

Submunitions

Most of the submunitions carried in cluster weapons and dispensers are of the free-fall, hollow-charge warhead variety, if they are intended to be used against armour. They are generally stated as having a penetration capability, where figures are available, of up to 8in (200mm) of homogenous armour. Most of them detonate on impact, which means that unless they score a direct hit they are wasted

The most effective dispenser weapon currently in service is the MW-1, which can carry up to 4,536 KB44 anti-armour bomblets. It can also carry up to 873 MIFF anti-tank mines, which lie where they are dropped until activated by the magnetism of a tank hull, or the vibration from its tracks. It therefore has a much better chance of scoring than the top-attack bomblet.

A submunition called Skeet has been under development in the USA since 1982, and shows a great deal of promise. It combines an IR target sensor with a self-forging fragment warhead. When ejected from a scatter weapon, it deploys a drag paddle, and rather like a sycamore seed, wobbles earthwards. The wobble allows the sensor to scan the immediate area, and on detecting a likely target, it detonates, the shaped charge forcing a lens-shaped disc of heavy metal into a streamlined slug of molten metal travelling at about 9,000ft/s (2,743m/s) which is over 6,000mph (9,875km/h), in the space of less than 150 milliseconds. As can be imagined, this has great penetrative power, although details are not available.

A further submunition based on Skeet is the Extended Range Anti-armour Munition, or ERAM. This contains two Skeet, a central seismic sensor, and three microphone-tipped antennae. The approaching target is identified by a combination of noise and vibration, and precisely located by sound triangulation between the antennae. At the point of nearest approach, or at optimum distance, a Skeet is launched into the air to attack the tank.

Other future submunitions seem likely to use millimetric radar to acquire their targets. This is a passive detection form since all objects tend to emit at these very high wavelengths, in much the same way as they emit IR, or heat.

TANK BUSTERS

AGM-65 Maverick

Maverick is a small rocket-propelled weapon designed to make precision attacks on small hardened targets. Using the proven aerodynamic configuration pioneered by the AIM-4 Falcon, six variants have appeared to date, not all of which have entered service, but three of which are carried by fixed-wing aircraft in the anti-tank role. A product of the Missile Systems Group of the Hughes Aircraft Company, it was approved for production in 1968, and entered service in 1972.

The method of attack in all anti-tank Mavericks is the same. The pilot selects a weapon, which automatically starts its gyro running. When it is up to speed, the weapon is ready for use, and a cockpit light illuminates. The uncage switch is then used to remove a protective cover from the nose, and the seeker head of the missile, which contains a small television camera, transmits the picture in its field of view to a display in the cockpit. The pilot then pulls up briefly and acquires a target in the head-up display (HUD). He places the pipper on the target before glancing down to the cockpit display to fine-tune the aiming cross. In the hands of a skilled operator this takes no more than two seconds, although five seconds is the required maximum. With the missile locked onto the target, it can be launched, after which the aircraft dives away.

Lock-on is achieved through contrast, light against dark or dark against light.

MISSILES, ROCKETS, SCATTER WEAPONS

The early television-guided Mavericks ideally needed clear weather and bright sunshine for best results, as these gave conditions of the greatest contrast. AGM-65A was used by the Israelis in the October War of 1973, scoring 87 kills in 100 launches.

In typical Central European weather conditions, the maximum launch range of Maverick of around 10 miles (16km) is not a lot of use against tanks, since not only are they difficult both to see and identify at much more than 2.5 miles (4km), but the generally dull weather and patchy background makes achieving enough contrast a problem. This led to the development of the AGM-65B, with Scene Magnification optics, which allow the pilot both to identify and lock onto a target at a greater range than would otherwise be possible, although this must be done through the cockpit display rather than the HUD.

The most recent anti-tank Maverick to enter service is the AGM-65D, which uses imaging infra red (IIR), which became operational late in 1986. IIR gives better homing contrast in conditions of dust, smoke, and poor weather, and also permits night attacks to be made. Other Mavericks are the laser-guided AGM-65E, used by the US Marines and Navy for close air support, and the anti-ship AGM-65F.

Below: Four AGM-65B Maverick missiles about to be loaded on an 81st TFW A-10A Thunderbolt. This model is currently being replaced by the AGM-65D which uses IIR homing.

TANK BUSTERS

AGM-114A Hellfire

Hellfire is a laser-guided missile which is intended to be the main anti-tank weapon for American battlefield helicopters, and in particular the AH-64A Apache. A product of Rockwell International, it is supersonic, unlike most heliborne missiles, and has a maximum range about 50 per cent greater than most of them, although it is much the same size and weight. Apache carries a total of 16 Hellfires, and thus has twice the firepower of most other helicopters. The laser guidance is compatible with NATO designators, as was demonstrated in firing trials carried out by a British Army Air Corps Lynx in 1983.

Hellfire is more versatile than most other heliborne missiles, and can be launched in the indirect attack mode from a concealed position, at a target designated by a ground laser. It can also ripple-fire several missiles in quick succession at different targets using coded laser beams. The missiles will climb above obstacles before searching for their coded target, homing once the correct acquisition has been made. Control is by nose-mounted canard surfaces, and Hellfire can pull a 13g turn while at maximum speed. Time of flight to maximum range has not been released, but is probably about 18 seconds.

Above: A USAF HH-60 Blackhawk launches a Hellfire. The smoke signature could give away the launch position.

Apache/CWS

Apache/CWS is a joint Franco-German project by Matra and MBB to meet a requirement for a stand-off submunitions dispenser which will save aircraft having to overfly their target areas. Modular in concept, it is of box-shaped cross-section, and has small high-lift wings that extend after launch. Weighing about one ton fully loaded, its overall length is about 13.12ft (4m), of which a 6.63ft (2.2m) centre section contains submunitions. A strap-down inertial navigation system is programmed by the pilot prior to launch, and this guides the weapon to the target area. Apache/CWS is intended to hit both static targets such as airfields and vehicle concentrations, and mobile armoured formations, in the last case using smart or semi-smart submunitions. It is to be compatible with a wide range of submunitions, including the KB44, MIFF, MUSPA, STABO, LASSO, MIMOSA, and ACADIE.

The basic variant is to be rocket-powered, with a maximum range of 19 miles (30km), while an unpowered glide version with a 6-mile (10km) range is also to be developed in parallel. An extended-range 30-mile (50km) turbojet-powered version may also emerge, which will be 2.62ft (80cm) longer. Both powered versions carry terminal sensors for detecting the assigned targets. Dispersion patterns are to vary between 3,280ft (1,000m) long and 1,150ft (350m) wide according to the load carried. Development started in 1984; flight testing is scheduled to commence in 1987, and weapons should be available in 1989.

MISSILES, ROCKETS, SCATTER WEAPONS

Above: A total of 16 Hellfires can be seen on this Blackhawk; the AH-64 Apache can carry a similar load.

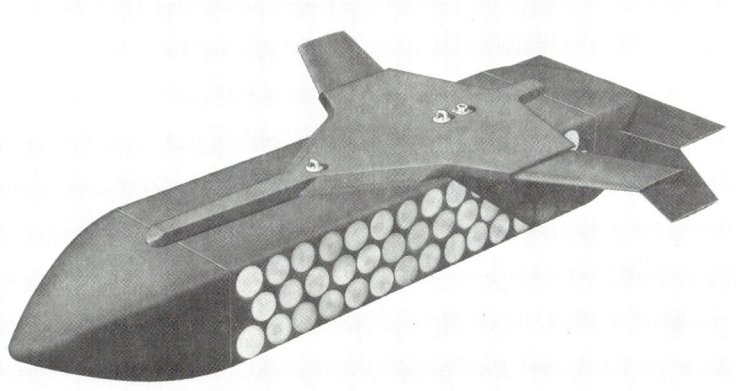

Above: Apache/CWS is a free-flying dispenser, with a rocket motor. It is pre-programmed before release. Both glide and turbojet variants are projected.

TANK BUSTERS

APILAS

A product of Matra-Manurhin Défense, APILAS is an acronym for Armour-Piercing Infantry Light Arm System. With a total system weight of only 20lb (9kg), it is easily man-portable. The all-burnt on launch (ABOL) projectile has a calibre of 112mm, and the hollow-charge warhead can penetrate up to 27.5in (700mm) of homogenous armour, while a special fuze design allows detonation at grazing angles as high as 80 degrees. The lightweight disposable launcher is very short in relation to the calibre, and is remarkable for an ABOL weapon, not only for its lack of length, but the fact that it permits a launch velocity of 961ft/s (293m/s), which is on the high side. Normally, the accuracy of unguided anti-tank projectiles, and thus their effective range, which is the distance at which they can reasonably be expected to hit anything, depends on the length/calibre ratio. The manufacturer coyly claims an effective range of 'more than 300 metres'. However, it is noticeable that in all photographs released so far, the operator is wearing an anti-flash mask. Be that as it may, the high launch velocity permits a flat trajectory over distances of 1,300 to 1,640ft (400 to 500m). The sight is telescopic, and can be changed to suit both left- and right-handed operators.

APILAS entered production for the French Army in 1984, and in late 1986 was selected to arm Finland, Italy, and Jordan

Below: The sighting system for APILAS protects the operator's entire face, necessary because of the high launch velocity.

MISSILES, ROCKETS, SCATTER WEAPONS

AT-4 Spigot

The AT-4 Spigot was first identified in the West in 1980, although rumours of its existence had been around for some considerable time before that. It is a wire-guided semi-automatic command to line-of-sight (SACLOS) system, with a similar layout to that of MILAN, although the Soviet missile is much larger and heavier. A man-portable unit, it is currently replacing the AT-3 Sagger in the Soviet Army anti-tank platoons.

The launch tube is tripod-mounted, and the guidance electronics are mounted below the launch rail. The sight is periscopic, which allows the operator to remain hidden, and appears to have two lenses, one above the other. It has been speculated that these are day and night sights, although to date this has not been confirmed.

It is believed that initial launch is by means of a gas generator, but conflicting reports indicate that the launch speed is higher than the cruise speed by a good margin. Both these reports cannot be right. On the face of it, Spigot is a very average weapon. If it has hidden virtues, these are not yet apparent to the West, nor are they likely to be in the immediate future.

Spigot is believed to have been used in action by Iraq in the late summer of 1986, although mostly against bunkers. It has also been supplied to Polisario guerrillas in Morocco.

Below: There appear to be two lenses on the periscopic sight of this Soviet AT-4 Spigot missile.

TANK BUSTERS

AT-5 Spandrel

Spandrel made its first appearance in public at the Red Square parade in November 1977. One of the larger ground-launched guided anti-tank missiles, its calibre is matched only by the British Swingfire. Too large to be easily man-portable, it is normally seen mounted in tubes on the roof of the BRDM-2 AFV, where it is mounted in fives on a trainable turret. It is believed that 10 reloads are carried. It is also mounted on the BMP-2 infantry fighting vehicle. Like the smaller Spigot, it uses optical tracking with wire guidance, with semi-automatic command to line of sight. The BRDM-2 has a rotating tracking head mounted on the vehicle roof to the right-hand side.

Despite its large diameter, the missile is not particularly heavy, being around the same weight as TOW 1 and only two-thirds of the weight of Swingfire, with its comparable calibre. Its range is highly speculative, but the generally accepted figure of 13,100ft (4,000m) seems to be reasonable, as anything less than this would make the AFV carrying it too vulnerable to the tanks that it was attempting to counter. Penetration is stated to be 19.68in (500mm), which seems a little on the light side for such a large calibre.

Two further Soviet weapons are known to have entered service; these are the AT-7, which is roughly equivalent to the American M47 Dragon, and the AT-8 Kobra, about which little is known except that it is fired from the gun of MBTs, and is believed to use laser beam riding guidance.

Below: The typical quintuple swivelling mounting of the AT-5 Spandrel is shown here on the roof of an APC.

MISSILES, ROCKETS, SCATTER WEAPONS

AT-6 Spiral

First identified as long ago as 1977, the Soviet AT-6 Spiral has only gradually supplanted the elderly radio command-guided AT-2 Swatter and the wire-guided AT-3 Sagger as the Warsaw Pact countries' premier air-launched anti-tank missile, but, unlike them, it appears to have no ground-launched application. Slimmer even than Hellfire, although rather longer, its maximum range has been stated as up to 6 miles (10km), but it is widely believed to be considerably less than this.

Originally thought to be a laser-guided weapon, it is actually semi-automatic radio command-guided with possibly IR terminal homing. The large hollow-charge warhead has considerable penetrative power, and the missile is credited with a kill probability of over 90 per cent. There have been persistent rumours that a variant using millimetric radar homing was under development, but this seems to have been one of the intelligence canards that occur from time to time, since no concrete evidence has been forthcoming.

Spiral is mounted in twin pods at the ends of the stub wings on the Mi-24 Hind E helicopter and it is widely believed to equip the Su-25 Frogfoot. It is, therefore, a reasonable assumption that it will be the main anti-tank weapon of the new generation of Soviet attack helicopters, and will equip both Havoc and Hokum when these enter service.

Below: An artist's impression of the new Soviet Hokum attack helicopter, which is expected to be armed with AT-6 Spirals, shown on the outer wing positions.

TANK BUSTERS

Belouga

BLG 66 Belouga is a Matra-developed weapon designed to give even scatter of submunitions over a pre-selected area when released at high speed and low level. A low-drag weapon, it carries a total of 151 66mm-calibre grenades weighing 3lb (1.3kg) each in 19 radially arranged tubes. Three types of grenade are available: fragmentation, delayed action, and armour piercing. The Belouga container is stressed to withstand up to 8g manoeuvring forces, and has a speed limitation of 725mph (1,167km/h). Release limitations are: maximum speed 635mph (1,020km/h), minimum speed 405mph (650km/h), and minimum altitude 250ft (76m). Prior to release, the pilot selects one of two scatter patterns, either 394ft (120m) or 787ft (240m) long, and between 131ft (40m) and 197ft (60m) wide. On release the container is braked by parachute to allow the aircraft to get clear, then the grenades are ejected in sequence. The launch tubes are slanted towards the rear; this and the fact that the submunitions are also braked by individual parachutes, allows them to drop nearly vertically. The submunitions are armed as their parachutes deploy, allowing the hollow-charge warheads in the anti-tank grenades to attack the top armour of any tank they hit. Up to six Belouga containers can be carried per aircraft.

Right: Two Belouga dispensers beneath a Mirage 2000. The black circles denote the submunition pattern.

BGM-71

A product of the Missile Division, Hughes Aircraft Company, the TOW (an acronym for tube-launched, optically-tracked, wire-guided), looks set to become the world's most popular guided missile, with more than 400,000 built to date in three versions, and further upgrades in the pipeline. Originally intended as a replacement for the 105mm recoilless rifle, it is now widely used by both vehicles and helicopters in addition to being an infantry weapon. It is currently in service with some three dozen countries, and has seen action in Vietnam, the October War in 1973, the Lebanon operation in 1982, the ongoing Iraq-Iran war, and against the Polisario guerrillas in Morocco. To date, over 24,000 practice launches have taken place, with a success rate exceeding 90 per cent.

Guidance is SACLOS, in which the operator holds the cross-hairs of the sight on the selected target, while an optical sensor tracks a light source in the missile (IR in early models while a xenon beacon is used in TOW 2), and measures the difference between the missile and the line of sight, then sends corrective steering commands along the twin wires. The launch has minimal signature, with little smoke or flash, and the missile is almost impossible to detect until just before impact, as demonstrated by target's eye view film, in which it can only be seen as it streaks past just overhead. Maximum range is stated as 12,300ft (3,750m), and the velocity of all versions is in the high subsonic region, both of which are just about at the limits of what is possible with wire guidance, one of the main limiting factors being the speed at which the wire can be paid out.

TOW 1 is the baseline missile with a 127mm diameter hollow-charge warhead. This was followed by Improved TOW (ITOW), with the same sized warhead but using improved compounds, and an extensible probe to give optimum stand-off distance at detonation. TOW 2 has a larger warhead, occupying the full 150mm diameter of the missile; it is also heavier, faster, and has an improved guidance link to overcome the degrading effects of smoke and dust. Other upgrades under consideration are TOW 2A, with an improved warhead; TOW 2B, with either a millimetric or EO fuzing to allow top attacks to be made, and a radio data link-controlled version with a greatly extended range and capable of supersonic speed. The warhead proposed for TOW 2A is stated to be of the tandem hollow-charge type, designed to beat the modern armour patterns. Fibre-optic guidance is a further possibility.

MISSILES, ROCKETS, SCATTER WEAPONS

Above: BGM-71 TOW is tremendously versatile. Launched here from an APC, it is also used by both infantry and helicopters.

TANK BUSTERS

CRV 7

The CRV 7 was designed by the Canadian Department of National Defense, and is manufactured by Bristol Aerospace of Winnipeg. It has a very high launch speed, which is intended to improve accuracy by giving a very flat trajectory, a long stand-off range, and tremendous impact energy. It is spin-stabilised to 40 revolutions per second by means of ingenious wrap-around fins at the tail, coupled with moulded vanes in the rocket exhaust. The warhead is a kinetic energy penetrator, possibly of depleted uranium, and three different types have been developed, their weights being 6.6, 10, and 15.5lb (3, 4.5 and 7kg), respectively. The basic rocket without the warhead weighs 14.5lb (6.6kg). The velocity varies with the warhead, but launched from an aircraft flying at a speed of

Folgore

At the top end of the market in terms of range is Breda's Folgore, with a claimed effective anti-tank range of 3,280ft (1,000m), or a maximum range of 14,750ft (4,500m), at which it would only be used against large targets such as bunkers. It achieves this with a boost motor which gives it a launch velocity of 1,247ft/s (380m/s), around Mach 1.12, and a sustainer motor which accelerates the projectile up to 1,640ft/s (500m/s). As an infantry weapon it has two modes; it can be fired from a tripod, which needs a two-man crew, aiming through a telescopic sight on the launcher; or it can be shoulder-fired by one man, with a bipod and a lighter optical aiming device, effective up to a distance of 2,300ft (700m). Various turret installations for fitting Folgore to AFVs have also been projected.

The launcher is on the long side at 6.0ft (1.85m), but this is probably inevitable to assure supersonic launch speed, while the length to calibre ratio of more than 23 should aid accuracy. The projectile is spin-stabilised, and the height of the trajectory is less than 10ft (3m) at 2,300ft (700m) range. Minimum range is 164ft (50m). The two-man version, including the optronic sight, weighs 60lb (27kg), while the lighter one-man system weighs 42lb (18.9kg). Folgore went into mass production in mid-1987.

MISSILES, ROCKETS, SCATTER WEAPONS

620mph (1,000km/h), the attained velocities are 4,100ft/s (1,250m/s) with the 10lb head and 4,900ft/s (1,500m/s) with the 6.6lb head. The rocket motors differ between the fixed-wing- and the helicopter-launched types; the fixed-wing rocket has aluminium powder in the mix and the helicopter rocket does not. The absence of aluminium powder reduces primary smoke on launch, at a slight reduction in impulse. The operational launcher is the 19-tube LAU-5003A/A, although the 6-tube LAU-5002A/A is generally used for training. CRV 7 is currently operational with seven nations. It is also stated to have a range of 11 miles (18km) in a ground-launched mode.

Below: An F-18A Hornet of the Canadian Defence Force lets fly with a pod of CRV 7 rockets. A very high-velocity weapon, CRV 7 features a range of KEP warheads.

Above: Folgore has a high length/calibre ratio which gives it long effective range for an unguided weapon.

TANK BUSTERS

GBU-15(V)

A product of Rockwell International, GBU-15(V) is, like the Paveway series, a modification kit which can be added to an iron bomb. Two base bombs are current: the Mk 84 and the SUU-54 dispenser, which carries a total of 1,800 submunitions. A cruciform wing and tail package is added to the base weapon, the tail surfaces having movable control surfaces. This confers good manoeuvre levels, and a glide capability which gives a reasonable stand-off distance of up to 53 miles (82km) if launched at high altitude. Two forms of guidance are available, which accounts for the '(V)' (for variable) in the designation. They are electro-optical (television), and IIR, the latter giving an adverse weather/night attack capability. They are easily interchangeable to give operational flexibility. In daylight the EO seeker can be locked onto the target before release; alternatively a data link module, working in D band, can be added to give an indirect attack capability. The weapon is released, and relays its seeker head picture back to the launching aircraft via the data link. It can thus be remotely guided from the aircraft, or can be steered and locked onto the target using the data link in reverse. The IIR seeker works in exactly the same way.

A further development, the rocket-assisted AGM-130A, will give a low-altitude release range of triple that of the GBU-15(V). A further payload bomb base for the system is the BLU-96 fuel-air explosive weapon.

HOT 1 & 2

HOT is produced by Euromissile, a company jointly set up by Aérospatiale and MBB. Rather larger and heavier than TOW, it is not man-portable, but is widely used on vehicles and helicopters, and has been ordered by no less than 14 countries to date.

Guidance is very similar to that of TOW, with the exception of the control system, which is a thrust deflector set in the exhaust of the sustainer motor. Another major difference is the propulsion system. Whereas TOW has a short burn sustainer motor which boosts it to high subsonic speed very quickly, HOT has a long-burn sustainer which gives it a lower maximum speed, but which takes it out to a range of 9,843ft (3,000m) in two seconds less.

MISSILES, ROCKETS, SCATTER WEAPONS

Above: A GBU-15(V) seen below the wing of an F-4E Phantom, with the AXQ-14 data link pod hung on the centreline.

HOT 1 has a 136mm diameter warhead with a penetration capability of 31.5in (900mm), while HOT 2 has a warhead increased to 150mm, with a claimed penetration exceeding 51in (1,300mm). This is of course against homogenous armour struck at a 90-degree angle; it is only possible to guess how it would fare against composite armour shielded by reactive armour at a less favourable angle.

Tracking has to continue during the missile time of flight, but in the helicopter application the machine is free to take limited evasive action from two seconds after launch, although this is limited to 6 deg/sec turn rate, 45 degree roll angle, and up to 1g side loading.

Below: Launched from cabbage-top height by a Gazelle of the French Army, a HOT missile speeds away slightly nose-up.

Hydra 70

The Hydra 70 is a lightweight rocket launcher by the Hughes Aircraft Company designed specifically for the use of helicopters, in particular the AH-1 HueyCobra and the AH-64 Apache. Two versions are available, one holding seven rockets and the other 19. The intended weapon is the 2.75in 70mm folding-fin rocket, with a variety of warheads. Both versions have the flat faces typical of helicopter launchers. Of aluminium construction, weight has been held to a minimum, and 65lb (29.5kg) has been trimmed off previous versions by the 19-holer, which with a combat load of up to four pods represents a worthwhile saving. Cost has been held down to a point where they can be considered to be disposable, but tests have shown that as many as 32 firings are obtainable without wearing them out. Firing is singly, or in ripples of two or four. Firing rate is half that of the Matra RL F1 and RL F4 systems, at just under 17 per second. To date, roughly 2,100 of the 7-tube M260 and 5,200 of the 19-tube M261 Hydra launchers have been delivered.

Low-Altitude Dispenser (LAD)

Currently under development by the American Brunswick Corporation, the Low-Altitude Dispenser (LAD) system is the answer to a USAF requirement for low-flying tactical aircraft to deliver submunitions on a variety of targets at stand-off ranges. Similar to but rather larger than the Apache/CWS described earlier, LAD is basically a glide weapon, although a rocket motor can be used to increase stand-off range up to 15 miles (24km) if necessary. Targeting is done by the launching aircraft using coordinates fed from the nav/attack system; alternatively an external source such as the Precision Location Strike System (PLSS) or external designator may be used. On-board synthetic aperture radar may be used by the launching aircraft to detect and identify targets. The dispersion pattern is extremely flexible, and both tube and air-bag dispensers can be used. LAD can carry out climb and descent manoeuvres, and also turn back to attack a target of opportunity that has been overflown. Manoeuvring can be either preprogrammed or inertial.

LAW 80

LAW 80 has been developed by Hunting Engineering in response to a need for a lightweight disposable infantry anti-tank weapon with a very high first-shot kill capability. The launch tube is extendable, being only 3.28ft (1m) long in the carrying position, for which it has a handle and a shoulder sling. Total weight does not exceed 21lb (9.6kg). To assist in aiming, the launcher tube contains a 9mm spotting rifle with five preloaded rounds of tracer with flash heads, which show when the weapon is accurately aligned. This is to make the weapon compatible with support troops, who will not be practised with it; it is also designed to be idiot-proof; the operating sequence can only be carried out in the correct manner. The range limitations are a minimum of 66ft (20m), and maximum of 1,640ft (500m) against armour. The hollow-charge warhead can penetrate homogenous armour up to 23.6in (600mm) thick.

Various adaptations of LAW 80 have been proposed; among them the LAW 80 Adder, which has extra equipment which allows remote firing, and LAWMINE, a LAW 80 launch tube with an automatic sensor which could detect tanks or heavy vehicles moving, firing when the target crosses the line of sight. Effective range was stated as 328ft (100m). LAWMINE has since been cancelled, but LAW 80 is entering production, and is to equip British Royal Marine and RAF Regiment units as well as the Army.

MISSILES, ROCKETS, SCATTER WEAPONS

Above: The Hydra 70 launcher's M247 anti-armour warhead.

Above: The M261 warhead holds a total of ten submunitions.

Above: The M255 warhead contains 2,500 flechettes.

Above: LAD is a manoeuvring glide stand-off dispenser.

Above: The man-portable, disposable LAW 80 being unpacked and prepared for action. It incorporates a 9mm spotting rifle.

TANK BUSTERS

MILAN

MILAN is a small and light system produced by Euromissile. It is portable by a two-man team, one of whom carries two missiles in their sealed launch tubes while the other carries the firing post, comprising an optical sight, IR tracker, and tripod mounting. MILAN is also widely used with a vehicle mounting, although it has no helicopter applications, mainly due to its short range, which is barely half that of TOW and HOT. SACLOS guidance is used, with control commands carried to the thrust vectoring vanes by wires.

Launch is by a boost motor, which fires for 1½ seconds, throwing the container tube backwards off the launch tripod, leaving it clear for a reload. At a safe distance, the sustainer motor cuts in, with a burn time of 11 seconds. Unlike missiles which have short burning motors to accelerate them to high velocity quickly, after which they are coasting, MILAN accelerates throughout its flight, although it is not particularly fast, and the time of flight to maximum range is quite long.

MILAN first entered service in the mid-1970s. In 1984, MILAN 2 appeared, with a larger diameter hollow-charge warhead, 115mm diameter as opposed to the original 103mm, and an extended nose probe. Penetration claimed for MILAN 2 is 39.4in (1,000mm) of homogenous steel. Reliable, accurate and cheaper than either TOW or HOT, it has been ordered by some 35 countries to date.

Mehrzweckwaffe Eins (MW-1)

MW-1 is a product of MBB, and is probably the ultimate in captive anti-tank submunition dispensers. Similar in concept to the British JP233 anti-airfield dispenser, MW-1 has a similar function as well as the anti-tank role. Since it is a captive dispenser it forces the carrier aircraft to overfly the target array, but it is the only one that is currently operational, and has been issued to the Tornados of the Luftwaffe. MW-1 consists of four sections each containing 28 tubes running transversely and open at each end, with a diameter of 132mm. In the centre of each tube is an explosive charge, the strength of which varies from tube to tube to ensure even scatter over a wide area. When fired, it ejects the submunitions on both sides at once, thereby negating any recoil forces.

MISSILES, ROCKETS, SCATTER WEAPONS

Above: As MILAN is launched, its container tube is thrown backwards, leaving the tripod clear for a reload.

While a mixed load of hollow-charge KB44 bomblets, MIFF anti-tank mines, and MUSA fragmentation mines is normally carried, a total of 4,536 KB44s can be carried as a solely anti-armour loading. The pattern can be controlled by the pilot, and ranges between 656ft (200m) and 8,200ft (2,500m) in length, and between 656ft (200m) and 1,640ft (500m) in width. As can be imagined, the shotgun effect is unsurpassed by any other weapon, either actual or projected. The wide lateral spread makes the weapon effective when attacking a line of AFVs at right-angles, whereas many dispenser and cluster weapons need an attack down the line, with its much higher attendant risks, to be effective. This, combined with the Tornado's demonstrated ability to make a blind first-pass attack at night or in bad weather, makes the MW-1 a formidable weapon.

Below: The intense scatter pattern of submunitions from the MW-1 dispenser carried on a German Tornado IDS. Both length and width of the pattern can be selected from the cockpit according to the tactical need.

TANK BUSTERS

Oerlikon SNORA 81

The SNORA 81mm air-launched rocket designation encompasses a wide range of weapons by mounting different warheads onto a basic propulsion unit. This is the TWK 006, a solid-fuel folding-fin rocket weighing 19lb (8.7kg), which at an ambient air temperature of 65°F (18°C), produces an average thrust of 11kN for a period of 0.85 seconds. If launched from a stationary vehicle such as a hovering helicopter, this is enough to accelerate the missile to an all-burnt velocity of 2,690ft/s (820m/s). From a fast-moving jet, this figure would be considerably increased, varying with the aircraft speed.

Panzerfaust 3

The need to keep infantry anti-tank weapons light and easily carried by one man calls for a small-calibre weapon, while the need to penetrate the heavy frontal armour of MBTs requires a large-diameter hollow-charge weapon. One method of resolving these apparently contradictory requirements is to use an over-calibre warhead in a small-calibre launcher, and the Panzerfaust 3, with its 60mm calibre launcher and 110mm projectile, is representative of this breed, which first emerged in World War II.

A further requirement met by the Pzf 3, and by few other anti-tank weapons, is the capability of being fired in an enclosed space. This is done by using the Davis countershot principle in which a mass roughly equal to that of the projectile is driven to the rear to balance the recoil force. In most weapons this recoil force is balanced by hot exhaust gases being ejected from the rear of the launcher at high velocity, but this means that the weapon cannot be used in a confined space, whereas the Pzf 3 can. Effective anti-tank ranges are 1,640ft (500m) against a stationary or a head-on moving target, and 984ft (300m) against a sideways moving target. An IR target marker fitted to the telescopic sight combined with IR goggles worn by the operator gives a night capability.

Right: The Panzerfaust 3 uses an over-calibre warhead to give high penetration for a low carrying weight.

MISSILES, ROCKETS, SCATTER WEAPONS

In the main, the warheads are of the high-explosive fragmentation types, with weight varying between 10lb (4.5kg) and 24lb (11kg), but the RAK 026/RAK 054 is a specifically anti-armour weapon, with the PHK 030 hollow-charge warhead containing roughly 2lb (1kg) of high explosive. Fuzing is electro-mechanical, and is triggered by contact, the maximum grazing angle being 15 degrees. The fuze is armed after 328ft (100m) of flight. While the maximum range of this weapon is stated to be 6 miles (10km), the effective anti-tank range is around 6,562ft (2,000m). Armour penetration is stated to be over 13.75in (350mm).

Below: A Westland Lynx salvoes Snora 81 rockets from the hover. The launch signature is very obvious.

TANK BUSTERS

Paveway II & III

The Paveway series of laser-guided bombs is typical of the breed, and the concept has been widely adopted around the world. First initiated in 1965, Paveway I was first used operationally in the later stages of the Vietnam War, where it achieved some success against armour, among other targets. Like all other systems, it features a laser guidance and control kit screwed onto the nose of an existing iron bomb, and aerodynamic control fins screwed onto the tail. There is no direct electrical connection to the parent aircraft, and the delivery mode is the same as an orthodox bomb. Paveway II entered production in 1977, featuring more advanced electronics, some cost-saving concepts, and folding fins which allowed more weapons to be squeezed onto the carrier aircraft. The size of the aerodynamic surfaces is matched to the weight of the baseline bomb; the guidance kit is identical in all cases. The range of weapons that can be modified vary between the 500lb (225kg) Mk 82 and the 2,000lb (900kg) Mk 84 iron bombs. Paveway II bombs are currently in service with 33 countries.

The Low-Level Laser-Guided Bomb (LLLGB) programme was begun in the early 1980s, and this is now known as Paveway III. This features improved scanning seekers, the latest microprocessor technology, and high-lift folding aerofoil surfaces to stretch the flight and give better stand-off capability. Texas Instruments is currently developing the software designed to control the angle of attack and of impact. The test programme will not be completed until 1988. Paveway III is currently only used on the Mk 84 bomb.

Below: A Paveway II LGB on a Buccaneer. The guidance pack is on the nose and control fins on the tail.

MISSILES, ROCKETS, SCATTER WEAPONS

RBS56 BILL

BILL is an acronym for Bofors, Infantry, Light and Lethal. First demonstrated in September 1985, and quickly ordered into production for the Swedish Army, BILL is a light, man-portable anti-tank guided weapon, which is extremely easy to set up and to reload. It can naturally also be vehicle-mounted. It uses SACLOS guidance, and the aerodynamic controls are operated via wire-transmitted commands. Maximum velocity is 656ft/s (200m/s) and maximum range is 6,562ft (2,000m). The missile is small and light, although its calibre is 150mm.

Thus far it appears nothing special at all. Yet it has attracted almost universal interest, including that of the US Army. The reason for the interest is that BILL contains some very radical features. The first, and most important, is that BILL is designed to attack the top of the tank, where there is not only a good chance of hitting the armour where it is thinnest but, even where it is thick, the angle of the attack is far more favourable than with a horizontal attack weapon. It also gives a far better chance of scoring a hit on a tank that is in a hull-down position. In order to do this, the warhead is canted down at an angle of 30 degrees, and is triggered by a proximity fuze. This has the disadvantage that the warhead diameter has had to be reduced to about 100mm, but there is an offset in that while hollow-charge design has increased its penetrative power considerably in recent years, it has done so only by ever increasing the optimum stand-off distance. The overflying attack profile of BILL aids this considerably. Correct fuzing is critical, but no details have been released to date except that the proximity sensor system reacts only to objects having the characteristics of AFVs. The control unit also has some unusual features. Whereas the trajectories of other anti-tank missiles are corrected to the line of sight, the computer in BILL actually predicts the missile flight path and corrects the actual to the predicted, while compensating for drift due to crosswinds. Counter-counter-measures have been included, while each missile has a specially coded laser diode beacon which not only makes jamming difficult, but prevents cross-interference if two missiles are launched at the same target on closely converging courses. Unless something springs a serious leak, BILL seems the way to go for the future.

Below: BILL combines a very sophisticated guidance system with a downward-angled warhead designed to attack top armour.

TANK BUSTERS

Rockeye II Mk 20 Cluster Bomb

A product of ISC Technologies, of Pennsylvannia, USA, the Rockeye II Mk 20 is smaller and lighter than most cluster weapons, but carries a total of 247 sub-munitions, which is more than any other weapon of comparable size. It is an unguided free-fall weapon, and is delivered in any of the modes that could be used for a 500lb (225kg) iron bomb, such as dive toss. The shapes and sizes of area coverage alter according to such factors as dive angle and speed, but in level flight at the release altitude of 500ft (152m), an area of 51,667ft² (4,800m²)

Swingfire

Swingfire is a product of British Aerospace Dynamics Group. It is very large, and is generally, although not always, vehicle-mounted. It features an indirect fire capability, with the operator stationed up to 328ft (100m) away, and its launch angle is upwards, which means that the missile needs to have no direct line of sight to the target at launch, but can be completely concealed. Its name derives from the fact that it can be launched at a target which is within 45 degrees either side of the launcher, and 20 degrees above or below its horizontal axis, the low launch velocity coupled with thrust vectoring control enabling the big missile to be pulled into the operator's line of sight at an early stage in its flight.

Guidance is manual command to line-of-sight (MCLOS) through wires, which calls for rather more skill on the part of the operator than the more usual SACLOS. The missile autopilot has gyros controlling pitch and yaw; when the operator centralises the joystick, having lined the Swingfire up on target, it will then hold its course until impact. The booster phase is unusually long at six seconds, but this is needed to bring the missile into the line of sight quickly; after this a long burn sustainer takes over. The sight is periscopic, and thermal imaging can be used to allow attacks in adverse weather or at night.

Right: The upward launch angle of Swingfire means that there need be no direct line-of-sight between the missile and its target; a fact that greatly aids concealment.

MISSILES, ROCKETS, SCATTER WEAPONS

is covered, roughly 328ft (100m) by 157ft (48m). Minimum release altitude is 250ft (76m) in level flight, and 100ft (30m) when the aircraft is pitching up. As all the bomblets are of the hollow-charge type, Rockeye is a specifically anti-armour weapon. Prior to release, the pilot selects a delay period for the fuze, which at a preset time after release sets off a linear shaped charge, which splits open the case, allowing the submunitions to scatter. The free-fall bomblets arm themselves in flight, and have fuzes that can discriminate between hard and soft targets, contained in a nose probe which gives the optimum distance for detonation on impact. Like many dispenser weapons, Rockeye has a long shelf life, claimed to exceed 20 years with only visual inspection.

Below: The Rockeye II Mk 20 discharges its submunitions when the casing is split open at a preset time after launch.

TANK BUSTERS

TBA Aircraft Rockets & Multi-Dart System

Thomson Brandt Armements of France are a major producer of unguided aircraft rockets, one of which has been the ubiquitous 68mm SNEB, used by many air forces. SNEB, or as it is now known, the TBA 68, is manufactured in a number of versions, which include high-explosive (HE), and chaff for radar jamming. The specifically anti-armour weapon, which is intended to be ripple-fired at the target, is the type 253ECC, which has a hollow-charge warhead capable of penetrating some 15.75in (400mm) of armour, and weighs 11lb (5kg). Rather larger is the TBA 100 range, the anti-armour variant of which weighs in at 84lb (38kg) and which is capable of 19.68in (500mm) of penetration. The effective range of both the 68mm and the 100mm rockets lies between 3,280ft (1,000m) and 13,125ft (4,000m).

TBA have recently introduced a novel variation on the theme called the Multi-Dart System, which, while it is not really intended to destroy tanks, can be effective against light and medium armour, and may well be upgraded in the future. The same rocket motors are used, but the warhead consists of a number of flechettes or darts, with a length/diameter ratio of 10:1. Intended for use from both fixed-wing aircraft and helicopters, stabilised aiming is not required, as the pattern of flechettes gives dense coverage over a wide area. Taking the 100mm type AB24 as an example, because this is the one with the greatest anti-armour capability: each warhead carries six flechettes of 24mm diameter and weighing 3.6lb (1.65kg) each, with a penetration capability of 3in (80mm) of armour. The impact velocity is around 1,640ft/s (500m/s), which is highly supersonic. Two TBA 100.4 launchers will enable 48 flechettes to be put into an ovoid-shaped area roughly 2,600ft (800m) on the long axis and 130ft (40m) on the short axis. (If this does not seem very deadly, consider that they will be travelling at a very shallow angle to the ground.) The smaller flechettes give a much denser coverage, as the use of 13.5mm darts permits a total of 36 per

Right: 68mm TBA rockets ripple from four pods beneath the wings of a prototype Dassault-Breguet Mirage 2000.

VBW

VBW is an interesting and unusual dispenser system under development by MBB for the Luftwaffe. Originally known as VEBAL/Syndrom, VEBAL is a contraction of Vertical Ballistic, and the weapon represents yet another attempt at hitting the vulnerable topside of MBTs, but unlike other dispenser weapons it relies on precision rather than area attack. Its ancestry lies in the World War II experimental SG 113A Forstersonde rocket mortar, which underwent trials fitted to the Henschel Hs 129, and consisted of a battery of six mortars firing vertically downwards, triggered by a photo-electric cell.

VBW promises to be a more reliable and effective system. It carries 18 warheads, believed to be the same calibre and possibly the same type as are used by the LAW 80 infantry anti-tank weapon, pointing downwards and backwards. The system has a sophisticated sensor package containing an IR linescan sensor, laser altimeter and radiometer, and a fuzing unit. During low-level flight, the sensors automatically scan the area ahead and to the side of the flight path for the target criteria, which are geometry, heat emissions, and metal. If a tank is positively identified, the computer decides which of the launch tubes is best aligned to deal with it, and fires at the critical moment. While the system demands that the aircraft overflies the target array, this can be at low level, the pilot concentrating on flying and surviving while the system engages targets of opportunity with single aimed shots. Service introduction should be around 1990.

MISSILES, ROCKETS, SCATTER WEAPONS

warhead, and 9mm darts a staggering 192 per warhead, which would give totals of 288 and 1,536 respectively in the same area, but as their penetration capabilities are a mere 0.59in (15mm) and 0.35in (9mm) of armour, they cannot be regarded as serious anti-tank weapons.

Above: VBW combines IR detection and an 18-tube projectile launcher to sense targets and engage them automatically.

Main Battle Tanks

THE BASIC design criteria for a tank have remained unchanged since 1916; only the technology and thus the performance requirements have altered. The three basic criteria are both obvious and well-known: armour protection, firepower, and mobility. What has been shown over the decades, and especially in recent years, is that different situations call for different approaches to the balance between these prime ingredients. The introduction into service of more effective infantry anti-tank weapons than the World War II bazooka, PIAT, or Panzerfaust has shifted this balance, as has the introduction of the helicopter as the second most effective 'tankbuster'.

The prime enemy of an MBT remains, however, another tank of similar capabilities. On the other hand, anti-tank guided weapons (ATGWs), whether carried by infantry, light armoured vehicles or helicopters, are inexpensive compared with tanks, whose cost averages something over $15,000 per ton weight at 1987 prices.

Although the Warsaw Pact tank force ranged against NATO in Europe is stated to outnumber it by around three to one, there is approximately a reverse ratio in the numbers of ATGWs. There is nothing strange in this. Western democratic governments have to account for their expenditure to their taxpayers, and thus manage to 'prove' (since any statistics can be perverted) that the ATGW is the more cost-effective weapon. The Warsaw Pact governments do not have to account to public opinion in the same way — so they have large numbers of tanks.

The very first tanks were 'land battleships' (literally, since the Army was not particularly interested in the concept so it fell to Winston Churchill and others at the Admiralty to see the initial project through). They were designed to break the stalemate of trench warfare in the second half of World War I, but were slow, lumbering, noisy, unwieldy, poorly protected vehicles, barely capable of traversing a trench, mechanically unreliable, requiring large crews and merely armed with a couple of naval 6pdr guns or a multitude of machine-guns. Their capabilities did not impress many officers on either side, but they scared hell out of the infantry, who had to face them crawling noisily out of the mist and smoke, and in the inter-war years there were wide-ranging discussions about the role of the tank in future conflicts.

There were to begin with two schools of thought: those who regarded the tank as an adjunct of the infantry, being basically a support weapon with speed limited to around that of a walking man, but sufficiently well armed and armoured to destroy enemy machine-gun and mortar positions, etc.; and those who saw them as a replacement for the cavalry's horses in the reconnaissance and pursuit roles.

Tank tactics

Two different breeds of tank were evolved in most armies as a result — the slow but fairly heavily armoured infantry tank and the fast but virtually unprotected cavalry tank. It took time for the idea to coalesce that if infantry were also given tracked armoured vehicles, so that they could keep up with the tanks rather than the other way round, a totally different form of armoured warfare could be waged.

The first nation to put this into practice was Nazi Germany, the secret of whose success in the early part of World War II lay not so much in superior equipment but in superior communications and deployment. Although France and Britain had tank designs which in several instances were superior to those of the Wehrmacht, both countries tended to split their armoured units up into small groups subordinate to the in-

From Centurion to Abrams, Challenger, and Leopard 2, the principal enemy of the MBT is still another tank, and armour, mobility and firepower remain the essential characteristics.

fantry, which allowed them to be destroyed piecemeal by the concerted German armoured thrusts.

There was a third breed of tank, the cruiser, which was usually fast and comparatively well armed but not heavily armoured — just like its naval counterpart — and it is from these designs that the modern, versatile MBT has evolved.

Rise of the MBT

The infantry tank has been rightly consigned to oblivion, despite such post-1945 monsters as the American M103 and the British Conqueror. The cavalry tank has survived in the form of light tracked reconnaissance vehicles, although more often armed with ATGWs than with an effective gun, and remains a viable weapon in a restricted role. The tank destroyer has almost vanished. This was a World War II concept in which an existing tank was converted to carry a heavier gun in a fixed superstructure, or a specialised vehicle was constructed featuring a big gun but thin armour — space and weight being the prime design considerations. A few modern examples survive, such as the West German Jagdpanzer Kanone, the Russian ASU-85, and the Swedish Strv 103, but basically wartime experience and post-war theory has led to the evolution of the versatile all-round MBT.

The first such design to enter service was the British Centurion in 1945, production of which did not cease until 1962, such was the soundness of the basic design. It combined the best features of the wartime Cromwell and Churchill, with thick, well-sloped armour and the proven 17pdr (76.2mm) gun. This was later replaced by a 20pdr ▶

Below: T34 tanks in Berlin in May 1945. The T34 achieved an admirable balance of firepower, mobility, and protection.

89

TANK BUSTERS

(83.4mm), and ultimately by the 105mm L7A1/2/3 whose excellence has been proven in war theatres from Korea and Vietnam to India and the Middle East, and which has been fitted to a number of other tanks up to and including the M1 Abrams. The Centurion's most serious flaw is that it lacks mobility, having a power-to-weight ratio of only 12.5 to 12.8bhp/ton, giving a maximum road speed of 21mph (34km/h), and in Israeli service it has been substantially uprated. Since 1962 the Centurion has been replaced in British service by Chieftain and latterly by Challenger but it is still in widespread service elsewhere around the world.

Soviet simplicity

Although Centurion was the first post-war MBT to gain recognition, it must not be forgotten that it was the Soviet Union that created the first tank that really fulfilled the criteria — the T-34. In this vehicle the brilliant designer Mikhail Koshkin, assisted by Alexandr Morozov and Nicolai Kucherenko, combined a first-rate 76.2mm gun (which was widely adopted in German tank-destroyers) with rugged and well-sloped armour, a powerful engine and wide tracks which gave it excellent cross-country performance even under extreme snow or mud conditions. It also possessed good battlefield survivability and the vital ability to knock out enemy tanks at long range, before their own guns became effective. The gun was the main consideration in the T-34's design and has remained so in its successors, the T-34/85, T-44, and T-54 family. Considerations such as comfort (not to coddle the crews but to reduce their fatigue level and enhance general efficiency) and communications have always been secondary in Soviet tank design. So long as the tank is mechanically reliable and can deliver a hard punch, Soviet designers are happy, and simplicity — which in turn means faster production and lower cost — has remained the keynote of all subsequent Soviet designs. The Soviet Army is able to get away with this design philosophy because its tank crews are virtually all short-service conscripts who cannot argue with the ▶

Main Battle Tanks

Name	Origin (User)	Overall length ft(m)
AMX-30	France	31.11 (9.48)
AMX-32	France	31.01 (9.45)
AMX-40	France	32.95 10.04
Centurion Mark 5	UK (Israel, upgraded)	32.26 (9.83)
Centurion Mark 13	UK (various)	32.33 (9.85)
Challenger	UK	37.94 (11.56)
Chieftain	UK	35.41 (10.79)
Chieftain 900	UK	35.44 (10.80)
Khalid	UK (Jordan)	35.41 (10.79)
Leopard 1	W. Germany	31.31 (9.54)
Leopard 2	W. Germany	31.74 (9.67)
M1 Abrams	USA	32.06 (9.77)
M1A1 Abrams	USA	32.26 (9.83)
M47	USA	27.93 (8.51)
M48A3	USA	28.52 (8.69)
M48A5	USA	30.55 (9.31)
M51 Sherman	Israel (originally US M4A1)	20.58 (6.27)
M60A3	USA	31.00 (9.44)
M60 High-Performance	USA	23.27 (7.09)
Merkava	Israel	19.69 (8.63)
OF-40	Italy	30.26 (9.22)

MAIN BATTLE TANKS

Width ft(m)	Height ft(m)	Engine power bhp	Max. road speed mph (km/h)	Range miles (km)	Main armament cal. mm	Ammunition type(s)*
10.17 (3.10)	9.39 (2.86)	720	40 (65)	373 (600)	105	APFSDS, HEAT
10.63 (3.24)	9.71 (2.96)	700	40 (65)	330 (530)	105	APFSDS, HEAT
11.02 (3.36)	10.11 (3.08)	1,100	43.5 (70)	373 (600)	120	APFSDS, HEAT
11.12 (3.39)	9.65 (2.94)	750	26.7 (43)	127 (204)	105	APDS, HESH, APFSDS
11.12 (3.39)	9.85 (3.00)	650	21.75 (35)	118 (190)	105	APDS, HESH, APFSDS
11.55 (3.52)	9.68 (2.95)	1,200	37 (60)	n/a	120	APDS, HESH, APFSDS
11.49 (3.50)	9.48 (2.89)	750	30 (48)	310 (500)	120	APDS, HESH, APFSDS
11.52 (3.51)	8.00 (2.44)	900	32 (52)	n/a	120	APDS, HESH, APFSDS
11.49 (3.50)	9.88 (3.01)	1,200	37 (60)	n/a	120	APDS, HESH, APFSDS
11.06 (3.37)	9.06 (2.76)	830	40 (65)	373 (600)	105	APDS, HESH, APFSDS
12.14 (3.7)	9.15 (2.79)	1,500	45 (72)	342 (550)	120	APFSDS, HEAT
11.98 (3.65)	9.45 (2.88)	1,500	45 (72)	310 (500)	105	APDS, HESH, APFSDS
12.01 (3.66)	9.45 (2.88)	1,500	42 (67)	290 (465)	120	APFSDS, HEAT
11.52 (3.51)	11.00 (3.35)	750 or 810	30-35 (48-56)	80-370 (130-600)	90	AP, APC, HEAT, HVAP
11.91 (3.63)	10.24 (3.12)	750	30 (48)	288 (463)	90	AP, APC, HEAT, HVAP
11.91 (3.63)	10.14 (3.09)	750	30 (48)	310 (500)	105	APDS, HESH, HEAT, APFSDS
8.73 (2.66)	9.62 (2.93)	460	28 (45)	168 (270)	105	HEAT
11.91 (3.63)	10.73 (3.27)	750	30 (48)	300 (480)	105	APDS, HESH, HEAT, APFSDS
13.75 (4.19)	9.58 (2.92)	1,200	46 (74)	n/a	105	APDS, HESH, HEAT, APFSDS
12.14 (3.70)	9.02 (2.75)	900	28.6 (46)	250 (400)	105	APDS, HESH, HEAT, APFSDS
11.52 (3.51)	8.80 (2.68)	830	40 (65)	373 (600)	105	APDS, HESH, HEAT, APFSDS

Table continued on next page

TANK BUSTERS

▶ designs they are given, and the Kremlin is happy because its Third World customers, unsophisticated in modern technology, can cope with Soviet products whereas their often poorly educated soldiery would be lost with many modern Western designs.

America did not have a viable indigenous tank design as late as 1940, despite a designer as talented as Walter Christie (whose concepts were adopted by both the British and the Russians), and was also a late starter in the post-war effort to develop a new MBT. Medium M4 Shermans and M26 Pershings soldiered on for many years until the interim M47 Patton and its immediate successor, the M48, came into service after the Korean War, and it has taken a very long time, up until the M1 Abrams finally went into production, for America to acquire an MBT equal to those of other nations.

Tank armour

A tank depends upon three factors for both its own survival and its ability to destroy enemy tanks. For protection, armour is the most important consideration, backed up these days by a nuclear, bacteriological, and chemical (NBC) system which can work either by means of filters or by internal over-pressure (i.e. sustaining the atmosphere inside the vehicle at a higher pressure than the outside air). However, each millimetre of armour thickness adds to the weight of a tank, increasing ground pressure unless the tracks are made wider, and reducing power-to-weight ratio unless a more powerful engine is installed. Both of these are important factors in determining a tank's cross-country mobility, particularly when the going is soft, and since mobility is of increasing importance in an age of 'fire-and-forget' missiles and helicopter-borne ATGW systems, tanks such as the British Chieftain may prove to be more vulnerable, despite their thicker armour, than, say, the German Leopard 1. It is advisable to say 'may' in this context because Israeli experience, particularly in the 1973 October War, seems to have determined that armour protection is more im- ▶

Table continued from previous page

Name	(User) Origin	Overall length ft(m)
Osorio	Brazil	32.79 (9.99)
Pz 61	Switzerland	30.95 (9.43)
Pz 68	Switzerland	31.15 (9.49)
Strv 103 'S-Tank'	Sweden	29.50 (8.99)
T-54	USSR	29.54 (9.00)
T-55	USSR	29.54 (9.00)
T-62	USSR	30.62 (9.33)
T-64	USSR	29.87 (9.10)
T-72	USSR	30.33 (9.24)
T-74 (T-80 to NATO)	USSR	n/a but similar to abc
TAM	W. Germany (Argentina)	27.01 (8.23)
Tamoio	Brazil	28.78 (8.77)
Type 59	China	See T-54/55 for other c
Type 61	Japan	26.88 (8.19)
Type 69	China	28.42 (8.66)
Type 74	Japan	30.88 (9.41)
Valiant	UK	31.28 to 34.85 (9.53 to 10.62)
Vickers Mark 7	UK	35.94 10.95
Vickers MBT Mark 3	UK (Kenya & Nigeria)	32.13 (9.79)
Vijayanta (Vickers MBT Mark 1)	UK (India)	31.93 (9.73)
XK-1	S.Korea	31.44 (9.58)

*Note only armour-piercing rounds are include

MAIN BATTLE TANKS

Width ft(m)	Height ft(m)	Engine power bhp	Max. road speed mph (km/h)	Range miles (km)	Main armament cal. mm	Ammunition type(s)*
10.70 (3.26)	7.78 (2.37)	1,000	44 (70)	342 (550)	105 or 120	APDS, HESH, HEAT, APFSDS
10.04 (3.06)	9.35 (2.85)	630	31 (50)	186 (300)	105	APDS, HESH, APFSDS
10.30 (3.14)	9.45 (2.88)	660	34 (55)	217 (350)	105	APDS, HESH, APFSDS
11.91 (3.63)	5.58 to 8.96 (1.7 to 2.73)	240 & 490	31 (50)	242 (390)	105	APDS
10.73 (3.27)	7.88 (2.40)	520	30 (48)	250 (400)	100	AP, APC, HEAT, HVAPDS
10.73 (3.27)	7.88 (2.40)	580	31 (50)	310 (500)	100	AP, APC, HEAT, HVAPDS
10.83 (3.30)	7.84 (2.39)	580	31 (50)	280 (450)	115	HEAT, APFSDS
11.09 (3.38)	7.55 (2.30)	700 to 750	43.5 (70)	280 (450)	125	HEAT, APFSDS
11.81 (3.60)	7.78 (2.37)	780	37 (60)	300 (480)	125	HEAT, APFSDS
n/a	n/a	n/a	n/a	n/a	125	HEAT, APFSDS
10.24 (3.12)	7.94 (2.42)	720	46.6 (75)	342 (550)	105	APDS, HESH, APFSDS
10.57 (3.22)	8.20 (2.50)	500 or 736	42 (67)	342 (550)	90	APFSDS
9.50 (2.95)	10.37 (3.16)	600	28 (45)	124 (200)	90	AP, APC
10.83 (3.30)	9.22 (2.81)	580	31 (50)	273 (440)	100	AP, APC, HEAT, HVAPDS
10.44 (3.18)	7.29 to 8.76 (2.22 to 2.67)	750	33 (53)	186 (300)	105	APDS, HESH, HEAT, APFSDS
9.94 to 10.17 (3.03 to 3.61)	10.17 (3.10)	915 or 1,000	38 (61)	236 (380)	105 or 120	APDS, HESH, HEAT, APFSDS
11.22 (3.42)	9.81 (2.99)	1,500	45 (72)	310 (500)	120	APDS, HESH, HEAT, APFSDS
10.40 (3.17)	10.17 (3.10)	720	31 (50)	373 (600)	105	APDS, HESH, APFSDS
10.40 (3.17)	8.66 (2.64)	800	29.8 (48)	300 (480)	105	APDS, HESH, APFSDS
11.88 (3.62)	7.38 (2.25)	1,184	n/a	n/a	105	APDS, HEAT, APFSDS

all tanks can also fire HE, smoke, illuminating, fragmentation, and practice rounds.

TANK BUSTERS

Above: The M1 Abrams demonstrates its mobility over tough terrain during its proving trials.

portant than mobility, as shown in the design of the Merkava. However, the Israelis' Arab enemies lacked modern ATGWs and helicopter tank-destroyers, so in the context of a European World War III battlefield the survival characteristics of an MBT may well be different.

The invention of compound or composite armour by Britain's Fighting Vehicle Research & Development Establishment (FVRDE) at Chobham in the 1970s heralded a new era in tank design. Although its precise composition is a closely guarded secret, it is known to be a laminate of titanium, nylon micromesh, ceramics, and probably other ingredients, which confers a very high degree of protection against chemical energy (shaped-charge) projectiles such as ATGWs and high-explosive anti-tank (HEAT) rounds, and will slow down even tungsten and depleted uranium armour-piercing fin-stabilised discarding sabot (APFSDS) rounds. 'Chobham armour' (as it has come to be called) is said to confer approximately three times more protection per millimetre of thickness than conventional armour plate. This means that the frontal armour on the Abrams, Challenger, and Leopard 2 is probably the equivalent in protective value to over 24in (600mm) of conventional steel plate — or even more.

Even more recently the Israelis have developed a new form of 'reactive' armour called Blazer which, interestingly, they bolt onto the turret tops of their tanks as well as the vehicles' fronts and sides. Traditionally, the upper surfaces of a tank have been the most thinly armoured areas because the threat has been mainly in the horizontal plane, from tank and anti-tank guns, or from underneath, from mines. Recent developments in artillery, such as the American Sense-And-Destroy Armour (SADARM) system described later, mean that tanks are now vulnerable to attack from directly above, but reactive armour may be a cheap and effective means of dissipating this threat. Soviet T-62s and T-72s have recently been fitted with reactive armour panels, while the older T-55s have been observed with large welded-on slabs, probably of conventional steel, above and to either side of the gun mantlet; this

MAIN BATTLE TANKS

has been nicknamed 'horseshoe armour' by Western commentators.

Fire protection

External protection is only one factor in giving a tank battlefield survivability. Fire is a constant hazard, both from HEAT rounds which 'inject' a stream of molten plasma into a tank as well as from the tank's internal fuel and ammunition stowage. As a result all modern tanks have fully automatic and rapidly reacting extinguisher systems, while an almost universal switch from petrol to diesel fuel further reduces the fire risk. Self-sealing fuel tanks and individual stowage for propellant rounds in compartments filled with water or glycol are extra protective measures, as is the use of blow-out panels as on the Abrams.

However good a tank's protection, it is even better to avoid being hit in the first place. This is where mobility comes in. Even though no amount of jinking about will deter a modern 'fire-and-forget' missile, speed and the ability to turn quickly will make life even more difficult than it already is for the operator of an optically tracked wire-guided missile such as Swingfire or TOW. The following table of first and third generation MBTs from America, Britain, West Germany and the Soviet Union provides some interesting comparisons, showing that although improved engine techology has made the tanks of each nation progressively faster and more manoeuvrable, British and Russian designers place more emphasis on armour for their protection, while the Germans and Americans rely upon speed to get them out of trouble.

Tank	bhp/ton	Tank	bhp/ton
Centurion	12.8	Challenger	19.35
Leopard 1	20.75	Leopard 2	27.27
M48A3	15.89	M1 Abrams	27.00
T-54	14.44	T-72	19.00

As further protection, all modern tanks are fitted with a number of smoke dischargers as well as systems to emit dense smoke from their exhausts at will; while this gives a degree of immunity from visual acquisition, it does not hide the tank from IR detectors, and a more sophisticated system designated VIRRS (Visual and Infra-Red Smoke) is now being introduced. Another British invention, VIRRS rapidly throws out a number of small air-bursting submunitions which almost instantaneously provide a cloud of 'hot' smoke through which the IR signatures of the tank's hot engine and gun barrel cannot easily be pinpointed.

Main armament

A tank's ability to survive on the battlefield is of course affected by its ability to do unto others — but first — what they are trying to do in return, so the main armament is in effect a defensive as well as an offensive weapon. The earliest tank guns fired solid shot (although most had an HE capability as well), relying upon muzzle velocity to impart a high kinetic energy and barrel rifling to impart spin to keep the projectiles on a flat and accurate course. Rifled guns on modern tanks do exactly the same but more usually use sub-calibre rounds contained within a sabot which is discarded as the projectile leaves the muzzle (armour-piercing discarding sabot — APDS). This gives very high muzzle velocity; for example, in the case of the Chieftain's and Challenger's 120mm L11A1 gun, 4,500ft/s (1,370m/s), ▶

TANK BUSTERS

with commensurate penetrating power, especially using high-density metals such as tungsten or depleted uranium. High velocity is essential since kinetic energy is a function of the square of velocity multiplied by half the mass of the projectile.

Although Britain has persevered with the rifled gun, largely undoubtedly to its accuracy, other nations have increasingly turned towards smoothbore guns which fire either fin-stabilised projectiles or HEAT rounds. The effectiveness of HEAT rounds is, in fact, adversely affected by the spin imparted by a rifled barrel. Smoothbore guns are lighter and cheaper to manufacture and have a longer barrel life than rifled weapons, which accounts for their popularity. The Soviet Union has fitted smoothbore guns to its tanks from the T-62 onwards, while late production Leopard 2s and the M1A1 Abrams are similarly equipped.

Rifled guns

However, smoothbore guns are not as accurate as rifled ones, and the individual rounds of ammunition are more expensive, so now that the FVRDE has developed an APFSDS round whose sabot is encased in plastic driving rings, so that it can be fired from a rifled barrel, the pendulum may well swing the other way again. Certainly it is no secret that Britain is working on a new hi-tech 120mm rifled gun to be retrofitted to Chieftain and Challenger, and it would be no surprise to see this on Leopard and Abrams in due course. All modern gun barrels are, of course, enveloped in thermal sleeves which reduce expansion, contraction, or 'droop' due to outside temperatures, which would otherwise affect accuracy.

It goes without saying that any gun has to be aimed, regardless of its inherent accuracy, and it is in this sphere that some of the greatest advances of recent years have been made, whether the gun is aimed by means of optical sights, a ranging machine-gun or a laser rangefinder. Auto-stabilisation in azimuth and elevation so that the gun can be tracked accurately regardless of whether the firing tank is rolling and pitching or the target is itself moving has been commonplace for many years, although surprisingly is still not fitted to French tanks. With early (and some current) systems, all the gunner had to do was hold the target in his optical sights to be assured of something like a 50 per cent first hit probability.

Later came the ranging machine-gun, which proved that the gun was on target and increased the probability to around 70 per cent, and most recently the laser, which increases the chances to 90 per cent when coupled with a ballistic fire-control computer. The most sophisticated of these, as fitted to Challenger, automatically assesses and processes every piece of relevant data, from the pitch, toss and speed of the opposing vehicle, through wind strength and direction, humidity, the type of ammunition in the gun's breech, and even barrel wear depending upon how many rounds have been fired.

In some tanks the commander can separately track a second target while his gunner is engaging a first, and then manually override so that the turret traverses smoothly within seconds to fire another round (pre-selected on the computer). Such sophisticated systems are, however, very expensive, which is why not all of even the latest tanks are fully equipped with them, and various compromises are introduced.

Future developments

What of the future? Pundits have been saying that the tank is obsolete for at least as long as they have been claiming that the manned combat aircraft is also a dodo, but saner minds know that there is no replacement for the man on the spot, regardless of how 'smart' a bomb, artillery shell or missile may be. It also takes human judgment to seize and hold objectives and to alter the course of a battle or campaign to take changing circumstances into account, so the tank is far from dead — although its shape will undoubtedly change.

One of the most interesting projects currently being investigated is a new American tank whose crew of three would all be well protected in

MAIN BATTLE TANKS

Above: Type 74 tanks on parade. Note the large white light/IR searchlight mounted on top of the turret.

the hull, while a very small turret would merely house the gun, breech and top half of an automatic loader. Instead of looking out through vulnerable armoured glass vision slits or periscopes, the crew would use high resolution closed-circuit television cameras. Upper surfaces would be heavily protected against vertical attack weapons.

Amongst other projects under development or at the prototype stage are the Brazilian Osorio, a conventional tank designed to replace the Tamoio. The latter is by modern standards a lightweight at only 29.5 tons, and only mounts a 90mm gun, whereas the new design will be some 10 tons heavier but with an engine of 1,000 instead of only 500bhp, and will mount a 105mm gun. The French have an EPC (Engin Principal de Combat) project in hand which is again of conventional design but will probably feature reactive armour, a powerful 1,500bhp engine and a 120mm smoothbore gun. Japan is looking at a replacement for the Type 74 which will feature a similar adjustable suspension (but only longitudinally), laminate armour and, again, a 120mm smoothbore gun, possibly with an automatic loader; this is designated STC or TK-X. The South Korean XK-1, designed with American help, is now in production and incorporates several of the features of the Teledyne High Performance M60 project. It has a powerful 1,200bhp engine, hydropneumatic suspension like the Japanese STC project, but for armament the venerable 105mm gun of British origin. Spain is considering a German design which is essentially a lighter Leopard 2, designated Lince.

Sophisticated electronics

It is probable that the next generation of tanks will be lighter and more mobile than current designs and may well incorporate more sophisticated electronics and IR countermeasures equipment to defeat 'smart' weapons. Other changes may well include automatic machinery so that reloading and refuelling can be accomplished on a contaminated battlefield without exposing the crew, while tank ammunition of the SADARM type seems likely. Inertial navigation systems, passive identification friend-or-foe (IFF) and improved crew conditions to enable a tank to remain 'buttoned-up' for prolonged periods are likely, and it is certain that a great deal of research is being conducted into ways of negating laser rangefinders and target markers.

By that time, of course, there will be new weapons as well, so the battle of wits between tank designers and tankbuster designers will enter yet another round!

AMX-30, -30 B2, -32 and -40

For over a decade following World War II France relied on American tanks for self-defence, but in 1958 design work started, in collaboration with West Germany, on a new MBT. After comparative trials of the rival designs, Germany decided to proceed with Leopard, and France with the four-man AMX-30 — Atelier de Construction d'Issy-les-Moulineaux (the suffix denotes a vehicle in the 30-ton class). In taking this option the French demonstrated their preference for a tank in which mobility was the prime consideration, armament and armour taking second place. Average cross-country speed is a respectable 22-25mph (35-40km/h). One oddity of the AMX-30 is that it has a co-axial 20mm cannon alongside its main CN-105-F1 gun instead of the usual machine-gun, but this would undoubtedly be useful against lighter armoured vehicles, saving the 47 rounds of 105mm ammunition carried for enemy MBTs. Muzzle velocity varies from 3,280ft/s (1,000m/s) with HEAT to 5,000ft/s (1,525m/s) with APFSDS, and despite the fact that its gun lacks auto-stabilisation, the tank has been widely exported. Effective range is 2,735-3,280yd (2,500-3,000m) and rate of fire is some eight rounds per minute.

In 1979 a modernised version was announced, designated AMX-30 B2, which has a laser rangefinder and fully integrated fire-control system (IFCS), improvements to the transmission, and low light television equipment in addition to the AMX-30's standard white light IR searchlight. However, the AMX-30 B2's IFCS is not fully automatic and has to be programmed manually each day, and the gun is still not auto-stabilised.

Strangely, the above also applies to the AMX-32 which was first demonstrated in 1981. In other ways, however, this new vehicle is a great improvement, featuring a more powerful engine to give it improved mobility despite a weight increase from 35.42 to 38.37 tons, and a redesigned turret and glacis constructed of laminate armour (although this is not believed to be as ef-

Centurion (Upgraded)

Sometimes nicknamed 'Ben Gurion', the upgraded Centurion entered service with the Israeli Defence Forces (IDF) in 1970, 11 years after the basic British Mark 5 upon which it is based. The four-man Centurion has always been a popular tank with its crews due to its good armour protection (up to 6in/152mm) and the excellence of the L7 105mm gun, but the Israeli Army considered its cross-country performance and range poor, so one of the most immediate alterations was from the British Meteor petrol to a Teledyne Continental diesel engine, which gave a 25 per cent increase in speed and 100 per cent increase in range, as well as reducing fire risk and enhancing reliability. This slightly raised the height of the rear of the tank, but Israeli vehicles are rarely seen retreating! Considering the age of the basic design, Centurion has served the IDF well, although to begin with there were criticisms that it was more complicated to maintain than the so-called Super Sherman. Other modifications have included larger fuel tanks, improved fire-fighting and optical equipment and a better ammunition layout permitting stowage of 72 rounds compared with 65 in the original vehicle.

The most recent addition, first seen in Lebanon in 1982, has been the application of reactive armour plates to improve the tank's battlefield survivability against ATGWs. This almost certainly dates back to the 1973 October War when Israeli tanks suffered heavily from these light, manportable weapons in Egyptian hands. Called 'Blazer', reactive armour is an invention of Rafael Armament Development Authority and confers a high degree of protection against such missiles; similar plates have been seen recently on Soviet tanks so it seems likely that it will be widely adopted.

MAIN BATTLE TANKS

fective as the Chobham type). The searchlight has been removed and the number of smoke dischargers on the turret increased from four to six.

In 1983 a further vehicle was announced, intended for the export market. The AMX-40 has torsion bar suspension like the AMX-30 series but is otherwise a brand new vehicle with a 25 per cent improvement in power-to-weight ratio, wider tracks to further aid cross-country mobility, laminate armour, and a 120mm smoothbore gun of French design for which 37 rounds can be carried. This has a range of up to 10,940yd (10,000m) with HEAT, and can also fire an APFSDS round.

Variants of the AMX-30 series include a wide variety of engineer and AA vehicles, a Pluton nuclear-missile launcher, and a 155mm SP howitzer.

Above: AMX-30 B2 being put through its paces in North Africa. Note the thermal sleeve completely encasing the gun barrel.

Above: Israeli Centurion on the Golan Heights, the location for some of its greatest — and bloodiest — victories.

TANK BUSTERS

FV4030/4 Challenger

Even though it shares a large number of other features with Chieftain, Challenger is very much a third generation design, benefiting from both thick and well-sloped Chobham armour (which probably gives it effective protection equivalent to 24in/610mm of conventional plate), and from the vastly superior Rolls-Royce Condor engine which has almost twice the power of the L60 and gives the tank a power-to-weight ratio almost 50 per cent better than that of Chieftain. This enhances cross-country mobility enormously and reduces the breakdown rate. It also has Hydrostrut suspension to replace the Horstmann gear on the Chieftain, which already gives a very smooth ride.

Challenger was originally designed as the Shir 2 for Iran, but following the coup which deposed the Shah, in July 1980 it was announced that the British Army would receive the new vehicle instead. Over 300 have since been produced and are in front-line service with the British Army of the Rhine (BAOR), where their qualities compared with Chieftain are greatly appreciated. Challenger has the same 120mm L11A5 gun as on Chieftain, although ammunition stowage has been reduced to 50 rounds, but it is expected that a new hi-tech gun of the same calibre will eventually be retrofitted. Challenger has improved vision equipment for the commander — the Thermal Imaging Surveillance and Gun Sighting System (which is being retrofitted on Chieftain) — and a state-of-the-art IFCS in which valves have been replaced by solid-state components, the emphasis again being on reliability. An armoured repair and recovery version is just entering production.

MAIN BATTLE TANKS

Above: One of the first Challengers to reach the British Army of the Rhine. Note the low silhouette.

Below: A notable feature of this FV4030/3 prototype undergoing trials is the well-sloped Chobham armour.

TANK BUSTERS

FV4201 Chieftain

Although a second generation post-war MBT resulting from a requirement for a Centurion replacement in 1958, the four-man Chieftain — which first entered service nine years later after a variety of teething troubles had been more or less overcome — is still 20 years later one of the most powerful tanks in NATO's armoury and the mainstay of the BAOR. Despite being designed at a time when the ATGW was in its relative infancy, it has good armour protection and one of the best guns in the world in the form of the 120mm L11A5, even though the latter has not been as widely adopted by other nations as has the earlier brilliant 105mm L7 and its derivatives. The L11A5 fires HESH at 2,200ft/s (670m/s) or tungsten APDS at 4,500ft/s (1,370m/s) and its GEC-Marconi 12-12P IFCS gun-control equipment coupled to a Barr and Stroud laser rangefinder gives it a 90 per cent first-hit probability at all effective battlefield ranges (approximately 3,800yd/3,500m), making Chieftain a potent tankbuster by any standards. Up to 64 rounds of 120mm ammunition can be carried, and a good crew can fire up to ten rounds per minute for a limited period. Chieftain's internal computer assesses everything from range and bearing of target to the tank's own movement, wind direction and strength, outside temperature, and even barrel wear depending on the number of rounds it has fired, and constantly feeds this automatically to both gunner and commander (who has an override control and can fire independently).

Firepower was the principal consideration in Chieftain's design, partly as a result of wartime experience when British tanks were always under-gunned compared with their German contemporaries, and partly because of the success of the 105mm weapon on Centurion. Even though its armour may not be as thick (the figures are still classified) as that on contemporary Soviet MBTs, its sharp angles and curves with few 'shot traps' (at least frontally) give the tank a high degree of protection.

Right: A Chieftain flying West German pennants during an exercise on the sandy soil at Sennelager.

Below: Two British Chieftains displaying powerful 120mm rifled guns protruding from their well-rounded turrets.

MAIN BATTLE TANKS

The vehicle's main shortcoming has always been its Leyland L60 multi-fuel power pack which, even in its current Mk 8A version, does not give Chieftain the battlefield manoeuvrability or reliability required, and despite numerous modifications over the years breakdowns are more frequent than the Army would like. Fortunately, like most modern AFVs, Chieftain was so designed that the complete engine pack can be removed and replaced within 45 minutes by a Royal Engineers FV434.

The tank has both an ordinary and an IR searchlight, co-axial and cupola machine-guns, two Clansman radios and a full filtration NBC system. Armoured recovery and bridgelayer variants are in service, and a replacement with Chobham armour superior to that on the Challenger, designated Chieftain 900, already exists in prototype form.

TANK BUSTERS

Leopard 1 & 2

First entering service in 1965, ten years after the Federal Republic was admitted to NATO, Leopard 1 was the West German contender in the trials which resulted in France going alone with the AMX-30 and Italy selecting the American M-60. At the time (two years before Chieftain and five years before T-64) it was unquestionably the best tank in the world; it has remained in almost continuous production ever since, albeit latterly just for export purposes. Although not heavily armoured by contemporary Soviet standards — indeed, its side and rear hull armour of 1–1.5in (25–35mm) thickness could easily be penetrated by a modern 30mm high-velocity projectile — Leopard embodied much of what German tank crews and designers had learned in combat against Russian tanks during World War II. The main precept was to build your tank around the best gun available because if you can destroy your enemy before he gets a shot in, you do not have to worry about your own armour thickness. Nevertheless, although choosing the British 105mm L7A3 for these reasons, the Krauss-Maffei concern did not neglect mobility, and gave the Leopard 1 a power-to-weight ratio of 20.75bhp/ton, compared with 20 for the rival AMX-30.

Leopard 1 is a conventional design sharing several features with its French rival, including a four-man crew, all-welded construction and torsion bar suspension, but its range and the extra rounds of ammunition carried (55–60, compared with 47) enable it to stay in action longer, and it showed itself superior in other ways to the French design during the comparative tests. Although early production versions did not have auto-stabilisation for the main gun, later ones have and the earlier vehicles were retro-fitted. Special spiked snow shoes can also be fitted, another result of 1941–45 experience. The engine/transmission pack can be changed in the field by a team of four men in only 20 minutes. Leopard 1 uses an over-pressure NBC system and has a dual white light/IR

Below: All MBTs have a limited fording ability and this Leopard 2 is no exception. Note the smoke dischargers to the rear of the Chobham-armoured turret.

MAIN BATTLE TANKS

searchlight, eight smoke dischargers and a co-axial as well as a turret AA machine-gun; however, the co-axial gun is not used for ranging purposes as in most other tanks of the Leopard's generation, the Germans preferring to rely upon a precision x8 telescope. A low-light television system for night use is available as an optional extra and has been fitted to several overseas versions, for Leopard 1 has been widely exported and is produced in several variants, including engineer, bridgelayer, and recovery vehicles as well as the well-known Gepard SP AA gun.

By 1969 it had become apparent that the joint programme between West Germany and the United States to develop a new NATO tank for the 1980s was not going to succeed, so Krauss-Maffei, as the main Leopard contractor, was given the go-ahead to design a new all-German tank, prototypes of which were manufactured in 1972–74. After extensive trials, including cold-weather tests in Canada, down to -50°C, the first of 1,800 Leopard 2s for the Bundeswehr was delivered in 1979. A new Rheinmetall 120mm smoothbore gun was chosen as the main armament, for which 42 APFSDS or HEAT rounds are carried. This gun can penetrate at 2,400yd (2,200m) the same armour thickness as can be penetrated by the 105mm L7 at 1,970yd (1,800m). Due to the size and weight of the ammunition rounds, a semi-automatic loader is incorporated. The Leopard 2 has spaced Chobham-style composite armour, full stabilisation, computerised fire-control system and Hughes laser rangefinder accurate to over 10,000yd (9,100m), as well as a thermal imager for accurate firing at night. Its MTU multi-fuel engine, one of the most powerful fitted to any tank in service today, gives an excellent power-to-weight ratio of 27.27bhp/ton despite the fact that the tank is 12.5 tons heavier than its predecessor; wider tracks and a longer wheelbase also reduce ground pressure, which is an obvious advantage in snow or mud conditions.

Overall, Leopard 2 is one of the top four or five tanks in current use, having both excellent battlefield protection and a gun equal of any. It will give good service well into the 1990s, which is one of the reasons the Leopard 3 project, initiated in 1985, has recently been shelved. The Dutch Army has purchased 445 Leopard 2s, the first of which entered service in 1983, while the Swiss have licence-built 380 under the designation Pz 78.

TANK BUSTERS
M1 & M1A1 Abrams

During the late 1960s the United States and West Germany attempted to collaborate on a new tank, designated MBT-70, but Congress eventually forced its cancellation (largely on cost grounds) so the Germans proceeded independently with Leopard 2. Between 1971 and 1973 numerous studies were made to determine the requirements for an American tank for the 1980s and beyond, and prototype contracts given to Chrysler and Detroit Diesel Allison under the designation XM1. Comparative trials between the two prototypes and the Leopard 2 were carried out in 1976, leading to Chrysler being awarded a three-year development contract, from which the first production M1 emerged in 1980.

The Abrams is powered by an Avro-Lycoming gas-turbine engine which gives excellent performance and a high power-to-weight ratio of 27bhp/ton, but has the drawback that when the tank is stationary the area around the exhaust becomes literally red hot, giving a very high IR signature which is not desirable on a battlefield. (It was for this reason that an auxiliary diesel was fitted in the Strv 103.) However, the engine is smaller and lighter than a diesel of comparable power and the engine pack can be changed in the field in under an hour (compared with four hours on an M60). It is also very quiet and does not suffer starting problems in the coldest weather. The tank has fully automatic transmission and torsion bar suspension which are both reliable and give a smooth ride.

Below: An M1 Abrams showing the typical slab-faced appearance conferred by Chobham armour.

MAIN BATTLE TANKS

Basic layout of the tank is conventional but it features very well-sloped Chobham armour giving excellent protection, especially frontally, from all known guns and ATGWs, putting it in the same class as Challenger and Leopard 2. The turret is fully stabilised in the horizontal plane but only the gun sight in the vertical, because of a cost-conscious Congress. The gun fitted to the M1 is the rifled 105mm M68 but the M1A1 has the Rheinmetall 120mm smoothbore; when production of the 7,058 tanks ordered is complete they will equip the US Army in virtually equal proportions. Both guns can fire an average of eight rounds per minute. A new depleted uranium APFSDS round has been developed for the M68 which will further enhance the capability of this well-proven gun. Either 55 105mm or 40 120mm rounds can be carried, the majority of them in the rear of the turret which is separated from the crew compartment by sliding steel doors. There are blow-out panels on top of the turret rear to protect the four crewmen if the ammunition explodes. A Hughes laser rangefinder, IR thermal imaging system, and a Canadian digital fire control computer are fitted to both M1 and M1A1, giving a high (90 per cent) first-round kill capability, although there is no provision (as there is on both Challenger and Leopard 2) for the commander to acquire a target and fire independently of his gunner, using an override control.

Overall, despite minor deficiencies imposed by zealous cost-control, the Abrams is a well-thought-out design capable of engaging the T-72 on equal terms.

Below: An M1A1 with 120mm smoothbore gun. One flaw may be the large area exposed to overhead attack.

TANK BUSTERS

M60A3

The M60A3 is the latest in a distinguished line going right back to the M26 Pershing, but like all post-war American tanks the M60 series has suffered from being far too tall for the modern battlefield — it has even been nicknamed 'Godzilla'! Derived from the original M60 which was itself basically an upgraded M48, and which entered production in 1959, the M60A3 started coming into service in 1979. It retains the American M68 version of the British L7 105mm gun after abortive experiments on the M60A2 with the 152mm Shillelagh missile system, which, being optically tracked, could not be fired while the tank was on the move. On the M60A3 the gun is fully stabilised (which it was not on the original M60) and modern refinements such as the Hughes AN/VVG-2 laser rangefinder, thermal imaging equipment, and semi-manual computerised fire control have been introduced. Up to 63 rounds of ammunition can be carried, and rate of fire is eight rounds per minute. Despite a 'Reliability Improved Selected Equipment' (RISE) version of the basic Continental diesel, performance is not better than in earlier versions of the tank and power-to-weight ratio is barely over 14bhp/ton.

Teledyne Continental have recently developed as a private venture a high-performance version of the M60 with a 1,200bhp diesel which raises maximum speed to 46mph (74km/h) and power-to-weight ratio to 23bhp/ton. It has a hydropneumatic suspension and new appliqué spaced armour which is said to render it frontally immune to high-velocity and HEAT rounds of up to 125mm calibre. However, so far only prototypes have been produced.

MAIN BATTLE TANKS

Above: An **M60A3** with its turret traversed to the rear during an exercise in West Germany.

Below: The clouds of smoke wreathing this **M60A3** do not conceal the high silhouette which is the tank's biggest flaw.

Merkava

In terms of armoured warfare, the Israeli Army is the most experienced in the world as a result of its numerous wars against its Arab neighbours since 1947. Over the years it has used a wide variety of tanks including the Sherman, progressively uprated and fitted with a 105mm gun; the Centurion which, in Israeli hands, has proved itself superior to later-generation Soviet tanks; the M47, M48 and M60; the light French AMX-13; and captured Russian T-54/55s and T-62s. This experience with so many different vehicles in actual tank combat has led the IDF to develop both its own tank tactics and its own ideas as to the principal requirements in a MBT, and these do not always coincide with those of NATO or Warsaw Pact designers and tacticians. A major problem Israel has faced over the years has been trade embargoes and other difficulties in obtaining necessary equipment for the country's defence, and like South Africa it has been forced to develop a large and sophisticated indigenous arms industry; Britain, for example, supplied two Chieftains for test purposes prior to the 1967 Six-Day War but afterwards backed out of supplying them in quantity. As a result, in 1970 Israeli Defence Industries commenced work on a new vehicle which could be produced independently of such restrictions and yet so far as possible share commonality of components with the existing M48s, M60s, and Centurions.

For some time rumoured to be called 'Sabra', the first prototype Merkava was completed in 1974 and shown to journalists in 1977; the Mark 1 began to enter service in 1979 and the Mark 2 in 1983. The vehicle's unconventional design demonstrates clearly that the main Israeli requirement was armour protection, and this has resulted in a vehicle very heavy for its size, with a low power-to-weight ratio of only 15bhp/ton (compared with 27.27 for the Leopard 2, for example). The well-sloped front glacis is constructed in two layers of armour plate, in between which is stored the fuel for the Teledyne Continental diesel engine. This system gives Merkava good protection against HEAT projectiles and ATGWs but is probably not as effective as Chobham armour. The engine is also at the front as a further protective measure, with the turret and crew compartment at the rear. The gun is the standard British 105mm as manufactured in Israel and fitted to other Israeli tanks, for which 92 rounds of HEAT, HESH, or a

Strv 103 (S-Tank)

Many people would say that the Bofors Stridsvagn 103 is not a tank at all but a tank-destroyer, since it lacks a rotating turret and thus has more in common with wartime vehicles such as the Jagdpanther, but the Swedes designate it an MBT nevertheless. Moreover, it is purely a defensive system, while it could be argued that a tank is by definition a weapon of offence. These considerations aside, it is a fascinating and revolutionary vehicle, despite the fact that its ancestry goes back to the 1950s and production ceased in 1971. Its virtually flat superstructure offers minimal area as a target and will deflect most anti-tank rounds, while having the two engines (one a Rolls-Royce diesel to keep all systems operational when the tank is stationary and the other a Boeing gas turbine for when it is moving) at the front gives additional protection for the three crewmen at the rear. Ammunition, 50 rounds of which are carried for the L7 105mm gun, is also stored at the rear, and it is unquestionable that the Israelis have used the same ideas in Merkava. There is an automatic loader so a crew of only three is required, but although the gun has a high rate of fire of 15 rounds per minute under ideal (range) conditions, it is doubtful whether this could be sustained on the battlefield for the Strv 103 has to point itself and adjust its hydropneumatic suspension to engage each fresh target. The latter raises, lowers and can administer a certain amount of 'twist' to the tank's alignment, partially compensating for the lack of a revolving turret.

A recent modernisation programme involves retrofitting all Strv 103s in service with Detroit Diesel engines giving 60bhp extra power, plus IFCS and laser rangefinders to replace the existing optical equipment.

MAIN BATTLE TANKS

new Israeli-designed APFSDS projectile can be carried. The gun is fully stabilised and the gunner has a laser rangefinder. Night vision equipment is also installed. Another unique feature of Merkava is that it can act as an APC for up to ten infantrymen in addition to its normal crew of four if the ammunition load is halved.

The Mark 2 has additional appliqué armour of the new reactive type on front and sides. This consists of bolt-on plates (rather like the tiles on the Space Shuttle) which explode when hit by an anti-tank projectile, dissipating the effect of a HEAT round and helping to deflect high-velocity solid-core projectiles. The explosion of one plate does not affect the surrounding ones, nor can they be 'detonated' by smallarms fire.

Above: The Merkava's small turret, virtually free of shot traps, will probably be duplicated on future tanks.

Above: An Strv 103 with its suspension lowered at the rear and raised at the front to give maximum elevation.

T-62

The T-62 has its own niche in history as the first MBT to be equipped with a smoothbore gun, the 115mm U-5TS, which, firing HEAT rounds, is capable of penetrating some 17in (432mm) of homogenous armour plate at around 15,000yd (14,000m). While similar statistics are not released about Western guns it can only be assumed that they are comparable. The same gun can also fire APFSDS at the high muzzle velocity of over 5,500ft/s (1,680m/s) but statistics show that this is only three-quarters as effective (13in/330mm penetration at 1,100yd (1,000m). There are compensations, though, because the HEAT round can only be aimed effectively at under 4,000yd (3,700m) while the APFSDS can be fired accurately at out to nearly 4,500yd (4,000m). As stated in the introduction to this section, however, neither HEAT nor APFSDS rounds from a smoothbore can be fired as accurately as an APDS projectile from a rifled gun, and the T-62 has not fared well in the Middle East against comparatively ancient Centurions or even M60s. A further drawback of the 115mm gun is that it only appears to have approximately half the rate of fire of the ubiquitous 105mm — some four rounds per minute compared with eight. The gun is fully stabilised but sighting is only by means of an optical telescope.

Given this poor performance, it is strange that Soviet designers have persevered with smoothbore weapons in the T-64/72/74. On the other hand, accuracy may have been increased by improved aiming equipment, as it has in the latest Western (excluding British) MBTs.

The T-62's lineage from the T-54/55 is readily apparent in its low height, well-sloped armour (especially on the saucer-like turret) of up to 9.5in (242mm) thickness, four-man crew, and transversely mounted diesel engine which gives a power-to-weight ratio of 14.5bhp/ton.

T-64, T-72 & T-74/80

Even while the T-62 was entering production in 1961 work had already commenced on a successor, which finally emerged in 1970 as the T-64, by which time work was well advanced on its own successor, the T-72, production of which commenced in 1972. Main differences between the two vehicles lie in the

MAIN BATTLE TANKS

Above: **T62s advancing in winter conditions.**

engine and suspension, the T-64 having a five-cylinder diesel giving a power-to-weight ratio of 18.4bhp/ton, the T-72 a V12 multi-fuel engine developing 19bhp/ton — both being significant improvements over the T-62. The T-64's suspension is hydromechanical while that on the T-72 is by torsion bar. Both vehicles have the usual Soviet cast saucer-shaped turret with frontal armour up ▶

Below: **A T-64 on manoeuvres showing its low silhouette.**

to 11in (280mm) thick, although there are minor differences between them, such as the position of the white light/IR searchlight, while the T-64 has the advantage that its 12.7mm turret machine-gun can be aimed and fired while the vehicle is closed-down.

Both vehicles have some form of compound armour on their well-sloped glacis, which is believed to be up to 8in (203mm) thick; even so the Israelis managed to destroy a number of Syrian T-72s in the Lebanon with APDS rounds from their trusty 105mm guns. T-72s have recently been observed with appliqué plates of reactive armour on turret sides and roof as well.

The crew in the T-64/72 has been reduced to three men thanks to the introduction of an automatic carousel-style loader for the main 125mm smoothbore gun, for which 39 (T-72) or 40 (T-64) rounds of APFSDS or HEAT ammunition can be carried. Maximum effective ranges are 2,300yd (2,200m) with the former and 4,375yd (4,000m) with the latter. The automatic loader at last gives Soviet tanks a comparable rate of fire to Western designs of some eight rounds a minute. The gun is fully stabilised in azimuth and elevation, a laser rangefinder is fitted, and the gunner has an image intensifier for firing at night.

A new Soviet tank is now known to be in production although little is yet known about it with any certainty. Designated T-74 by the Russians (and T-80 by NATO for some strange reason), it has an improved 125mm smoothbore gun, a gas-turbine engine as on the Abrams, and compound armour which is believed to have increased weight from the 40 tons of the T-72 to some 47 tons. No performance figures are available but it is believed the T-74 will be comparable in most respects to the latest generation of Western MBTs, with an automatic loader, laser rangefinder and computerised fire control, while a new APFSDS round, possibly with a depleted uranium core, is also thought to have been developed.

All modern Soviet AFVs have NBC filtration, while their crew compartments have a lead or boron lining to give some protection against enhanced radiation (neutron) weapons.

Type 69

The latest Chinese tank, which was first seen by Western observers in 1982, is basically identical to the earlier Type 59 apart from the introduction of a computerised fire-control system, laser rangefinder, passive night vision equipment (although this is being retrospectively fitted to the T-59 as well), and on some models a Chinese-made version of the British 105mm L7 gun with fume extractor; others retain the T-59's 100mm weapon although it may be an improved version.

The T-59/69 are both closely based upon the Soviet T-54/55, large numbers of which were supplied to the People's Republic before the rift between the two regimes in the early 1960s, and main armament until the introduction of the new 105mm has always been the M1944 100mm weapon, for which 34 rounds of ammunition are carried. This gun has a muzzle velocity of 2,950–4,650ft/s (900–1,415m/s) depending on whether HEAT, AP, APC, or HVAPDS is being fired, with a rate of fire of four rounds per minute. Armour penetration at 1,100yd (1,000m) is up to 15in (380mm) with HEAT. Effective range with the laser rangefinder is some 3,500-4,000yd (3,400-3,900m). Both the 100mm and the 105mm guns are fully stabilised in azimuth and elevation.

The vehicle shares the same layout as the T-54/55 with four crew members, a low hull, torsion bar suspension and transversely mounted diesel engine giving a power-to-weight ratio of 14.4bhp/ton. Armour thickness is up to 8in (203mm) on the front of the saucer-like turret. Over 1,000 Type 69s have been sold to Iraq since 1983 for use in the continuing Gulf War with Iran, and an armoured recovery version is also in production.

Right: Although it has computerised GM-09 IFCS, the Type 69 has to remain stationary for 3 seconds to aim.

MAIN BATTLE TANKS

Above: A T-72 with its different ammunition types on display.

TANK BUSTERS

Type 74

Japanese tanks had proven grossly inadequate during World War II, and when the Japanese Self-Defence Force was formed in 1950 it was equipped, like the German Bundeswehr, with American designs. Four years later design work began on a new indigenous tank which entered service in 1961, designated Type 61, but this was closely based on existing American vehicles and was so unsuccessful that work on a replacement commenced the following year. With the typical Japanese flair for imitation, this blended elements of the Leopard (welded hull), AMX-30 (cast turret), Centurion (gun), and Strv 103 (suspension), and finally emerged in 1975 as the Type 74. Like all Japanese tanks, it is comparatively lightly armoured, but the curved and angled plates are effective and the gun is widely known to be highly efficient and accurate. The crew is of four men. Like the S-Tank, the Type 74 has hydropneumatic suspension which enables it to be raised or lowered on its tracks to give ground clearance of between 8 and 25.6in (20 and 65cm), which confusingly makes it look like a T-54 or an M48 depending on mode! The idea is to give the tank a low silhouette in combat coupled with good mobility over soft ground, while it can also elevate itself, without moving, from a turret-down position to engage a target and then discreetly sink down again. This complicated system does, however, need a lot of maintenance to function perfectly and one wonders how long it would hold out in a battlefield environment.

The gun is fully stabilised and has a laser rangefinder and computerised fire-control system, while white light/IR searchlight, NBC protection and six smoke dischargers are standard fit. Over 800 Type 74s have been manufactured and an armoured recovery version has also been produced.

Vijayanta (Vickers MBT Mark 1)

When the British Army ordered Chieftain, Vickers Defence Systems realised that few 'Third World' countries would require such a vehicle, or be able to afford it, and independently set about developing a cheaper and lighter tank for export. The result was the MBT Mark 1 for which the Indian government signed a production licence in 1961, and which went into full-scale production in Madras in 1965. Since then an estimated 1,500 have been built, and various modifications — including Marconi IFCS and Barr and Stroud laser rangefinding equipment — have been installed, but despite experiments with both the Rolls-Royce Condor and a Cummins diesel, India has kept its production vehicles engined with the Leyland L60.

Vijayanta is a tank of conventional four-man design and welded construction

MAIN BATTLE TANKS

Above: From this angle, with its suspension partially raised, the Type 74's hybrid design ancestry is very apparent.

with armour up to 3in (80mm) thick, armed with the proven 105mm L7A1 for which 44 rounds are carried. At 37.98 tons it is considerably lighter than Chieftain or even Centurion, resulting in a power-to-weight ratio of 16.83bhp/ton compared with 13.49 and 12.8 respectively, making it very mobile and probably accounting for the satisfactory maintenance level on the L60 as well. Cross-country performance is said to be excellent and the torsion bar suspension trouble-free. Nevertheless, after the 1971 war with Pakistan, Indian tank crews have been reported as saying they preferred the substantial extra armour protection of their old Centurions!

Mark 3 versions of the Vickers MBT have been exported to Kenya and Nigeria, and experience with the design has led to the later Vickers Mark 7 and Valiant with Chobham armour and 120mm guns, although neither is yet in production.

Below: A trio of Indian Army Vijayantas showing the effective camouflage scheme adopted for desert and bush warfare. Limited armour protection is the tank's worst failing.

Light AFVs

IT COULD be said that any AFV has an anti-tank capability, even if it is only that of ferrying troops equipped with portable ATGWs into action, or acting in support of them and the MBTs. This section therefore concentrates upon dedicated tank-destroyers and other vehicles with intrinsic tankbuster capability.

As stated in the introduction to the previous section, the 'tank-destroyer' concept went out of favour with the end of World War II as the idea of the 'universal' tank became more widely adopted, but with the introduction of increasingly more sophisticated guided missiles a new breed has evolved. Initially such vehicles were merely existing designs, such as the French AMX-13 light tank or the British Ferret armoured car with ATGWs fitted as add-on extras, but subsequently a whole new generation of light, highly mobile AFVs dedicated wholly or partially to the tank-killing role has emerged. Such vehicles can be wheeled armoured cars, wheeled or tracked APCs or mechanised infantry combat vehicles (MICVs), wheeled or tracked reconnaissance vehicles, or, in a few surviving examples, dedicated gun-armed tank-destroyers in the conventional sense.

During World War II the tank-destroyer evolved through two routes. Either an existing tank chassis was adapted to carry a more powerful gun than its turret would permit, by means of discarding the turret altogether and fitting the gun into a fixed superstructure; or a special vehicle was designed with relatively thin armour to compensate for the weight of a more powerful gun and its heavier ammunition. Examples of the former include the German Stug III/IV, Jagdpanzer IV, Hetzer, Elefant, Marder, Nashorn, and Jagdpanther, the Italian Semovente, the British Archer, and the Soviet SU-76, SU-85, SU-100, and SU-122; of the latter the American M10, M18, and M36. With the exception of the SU-100, which is still used by Egypt and Syria although rarely these days in the front line, all of these have now disappeared.

The sharing of common components has become increasingly important as weapons become more sophisticated and therefore expensive, and nowhere is this more evident than in the current British Scorpion family. Scorpion itself is actually a light tank, although not designated as such, and its 76mm gun (for which 40 rounds of ammunition are carried) gives it a limited anti-tank capability, although being designed for reconnaissance this is not its major function. This is the role of Striker, armed with Swingfire missiles. On the battlefield Striker operates closely with Scimitar, which has a quick-firing 30mm Rarden cannon in a fully rotating turret, the idea being that Scimitar protects Striker from enemy infantry while Striker deals with the tanks. All three vehicles share the same engine and chassis, as do the others in the family: Spartan, the APC; Sultan, the command vehicle; Samson, the engineer and recovery vehicle; and Samaritan, the ambulance version. Spartan is itself now being fitted with MILAN launchers as are the venerable FV432 APC and the Fox armoured car, thus giving the infantry a measure of anti-tank capability. Striker has now completely replaced the FV438 which was for many years the British Army's dedicated tank-destroyer. Based on the FV432 chassis, the FV438 only had a single Swingfire missile launcher and this could only be reloaded from outside the vehicle — a hazardous and unpopular task!

Aluminium armour

Like most light AFVs these days, the Scorpion family has aluminium armour which is obviously lighter than steel but only confers one-third the protective value (i.e. 1 in/25.4mm of steel equals 3in/76.2 mm of aluminium). Aluminium armour also reacts badly to HEAT rounds and ignites spontaneously. However, it is more rigid than steel so can be used constructionally, helping further to reduce a vehicle's weight and enhance mobility.

Although the gun-armed tank destroyer has all but vanished, ATGWs give light AFVs a strong punch.

France has largely continued to uprate older vehicles such as the AML-90 armoured car and AMX-13 light tank. In the late 1970s, however, two new armoured cars were produced by Panhard: Sagaie and Lynx. Both are six-wheeled vehicles, ▶

Below: The AMX-13, a popular light tankbuster.

TANK BUSTERS

▶ the centre pair of wheels being raised when running on roads, and they are powered by Peugeot petrol engines. The main differences between them is that Sagaie has a smoothbore 90mm gun firing either a fin-stabilised HEAT round at 2,130ft/s (650m/s) or an APFSDS round at 4,430ft/s (1,350m/s) which are effective against most tanks at 2,200yd (2,000m); Lynx, on the other hand, has the same rifled 90mm gun as on the AML-90. Both vehicles can carry 20–21 rounds of main-gun ammunition. A projected heavy armoured car, AMX-10RC, was abandoned.

Combat experience

In America the emphasis until the M2/M3 Bradley arrived was on giving the M113 APC an anti-tank capability (the TOW-armed M901 performs this role today), but there were a couple of innovative even though unsuccessful attempts at designing other tank-destroyers. The earliest of these was the M50 Ontos which entered service in 1963 and eventually saw limited action with the US Marines in Vietnam. This was a light (8.5-ton) air-portable vehicle with a three-man crew, and very dramatic in appearance with its six 106mm recoilless rifles, three either side of a small limited-traverse turret. As usual, the main problem with recoilless guns was that they gave away their presence the moment they fired, due to the backblast. Having six pre-loaded weapons on a fast-moving vehicle was supposed to negate this disadvantage, but it is significant that they were all withdrawn and scrapped in 1970.

A vehicle which theory said should have had more potential than the Ontos was the M551 Sheridan light tank, which first appeared in 1966. Its specification sounded formidable, with a diesel engine giving a power-to-weight ratio of 19.26bhp/ton and good cross-country mobility, plus a unique 152mm gun/missile launcher capable of firing both HEAT rounds and the Shillelagh missile. The major problems with the latter were that only ten rounds could be carried due to its size and weight, and that although it was lethal against all forms of armour at up to 3,280yd (3,000m), it could not be brought in-to the gunner's cross-hair sight until it had already travelled 1,300yd (1,200m). This obviously made it useless in anything other than a relatively long-range battle, and after combat experience in Vietnam the Sheridan was also retired from service in 1970. (The same 152mm system was also fitted to the M60 in its A2 variant, but was equally unsuccessful.)

The Soviet Union has always specialised in light, fast tank designs as well as pioneering the MBT concept in the T-34, and has always put a greater emphasis on amphibious capability than have other nations. One result of this was the PT-76 amphibious light tank which is still in widespread service around the world despite being first introduced in 1952. It has been built in at least 15 variants and although it is gradually being replaced by the BMP-1/2 is still

Light AFVs

Name	Origin (User)	Overall length ft(m)
2S1	USSR	23.95 (7.30)
2S3	USSR	25.53 (7.78)
AML-90 (Eland 90)	France (S. Africa)	12.44 3.79
AMX-13	France (various)	20.8 (6.35)
AMX-VCI	France (Belgium)	18.18 (5.54)
BMP-1/2	USSR	22.15 (6.75)
BRDM-2	USSR	18.87 (5.75)
ASU-85	USSR	27.86 (8.49)
Commando	USA	18.64 5.68
EE-9 Cascavel	Brazil	16.90 (5.15)
Fox MILAN	UK	18.18 (5.36)
FUG	Czechoslovakia	18.87 (5.75)
FV432 MILAN	UK	17.23 (5.25)
FV438	UK	16.75 (5.10)
Lynx	France	17.85 (5.44)

LIGHT AFVs

in front-line service throughout the Warsaw Pact. Principally a reconnaissance vehicle, it is comparable to the British Scorpion in capability although less manoeuvrable, and is armed with a similar 76mm gun in a fully traversing turret which gives it a limited anti-tank capability. Although having no internal space for them, unlike a modern MICV, the PT-76 has a large, flat rear deck and broad mudguards on which to carry infantry, a Soviet practice going back many years. A surprising drawback on this vehicle is its large, forward-hinging turret hatch, like that on early T-34s, which renders it especially vulnerable when operating 'unbuttoned' and which cannot be popular with its commanders.

While the BMP-1 and -2 are not the latest Russian MICVs, there is evidence that the MT-LB has not been a success, and that the former vehicles, with an anti-tank capability through both a single AT-3 launcher and a 73mm gun (compared with the latter's single 7.62mm machine-gun), are still prominent in the Warsaw Pact arsenal. Introduced in 1967, the BMP has a crew of three and can carry eight infantry. It is low and fast with a power-to-weight ratio of 24.73bhp/ton as well as being fully amphibious, and an automatic loader gives its smoothbore gun a rate of fire of eight fin-stablised HEAT rounds per minute (a total of 40 rounds being carried). Only three AT-3s are carried internally, suggesting that their role is purely defensive.

There is still a great deal of debate about the role of the MICV, especially since the 1973 October War when Egyptian infantry attempting to fight from their vehicles in the front line with tanks found themselves sitting ▶

Width ft(m)	Height ft(m)	Engine power bhp	Max. road speed mph (km/h)	Range miles (km)	Main armament cal. mm	Ammunition type(s)*
9.85 (3.00)	7.94 (2,42)	240	37 (60)	310 (500)	122	HEAT
10.49 (3.2)	8.92 (2.72)	500	31 (50)	186 (300)	152	APHE, nuclear
6.46 (1.98)	6.79 (2.07)	90	62 (100)	372 (600)	90	HEAT
8.2 (2.5)	7.68 (2.34)	270	37 (60)	218 (350)	75, 90, or 105	HEAT or SS-12, or HOT
8.24 (2.32)	7.61 (2.32)	250	40 (65)	250 (400)	—	TOW
9.75 (2.97)	6.50 (1.98)	280	34 (55)	310 (500)	73(BMP-1) 30(BMP-2)	HEAT AT-3, AT-5
7.71 (2.35)	7.58 (2.31)	140	62 (100)	460 (750)	—	AT-3, AT-5
9.19 (2.80)	6.92 (2.11)	240	(44)	160 (260)	85	APHE
7.42 (2,26)	8.00 (2.43)	155	55 (88)	600 (950)	90	HEAT or TOW, etc.
7.94 (2.42)	7.55 (2.30)	172	62 (100)	460 (750)	90	HEAT
7.00 (2.13)	7.22 (2.20)	195	65 (104)	267 (430)	(30)	MILAN
7.71 (2.35)	7.58 (2.31)	140	62 (100)	460 (750)	81	HEAT
9.19 (2.80)	7.50 (2.29)	240	32 (52)	360 (580)	—	MILAN
9.75 (2.97)	8.88 (2.70)	240	32 (52)	360 (580)	—	Swingfire
8.19 (2.49)	7.99 (2.44)	115	56 (90)	590 (950)	90	HEAT

Table continued on next page

TANK BUSTERS

Table continued from previous page

Name	Origin (User)	length ft(m)	Width ft(m)	Height ft(m)	Engine power bhp	Max. road speed mph (km/h)
Jagdpanzer Kanone	W. Germany	20.50 (6.24)	9.75 (2.97)	6.83 (2.08)	500	44 (70)
M2/M3 Bradley	USA	21.18 (6.45)	10.5 (3.2)	9.75 (2.97)	300	41 (66)
M109A1/A2	USA	21.70 (6.61)	10.81 (3.29)	10.04 (3.06)	405	35 (56)
M551 Sheridan	USA	20.67 (6.30)	9.25 (2.82)	9.67 (2.95)	300	45 (70)
M901 (M113)	USA	15.96 (4,86)	8.81 (2.69)	8.20 (2.50)	215	42 (68)
Marder MILAN	W. Germany	22.25 (6.79)	10.63 (3.24)	9.39 (2.86)	600	46 (75)
Palmaria	Italy	37.66 (11.47)	7.71 (2.35)	9.43 (2.87)	750	37 (60)
PT-76	USSR	25.02 7.62	10.44 (3.18)	7.42 (2.26)	240	27 (44)
Sagaei	France	25.55 (7.78)	8.19 (2.49)	7.35 (2.24)	140	68 (110)
Scorpion	UK	15.71 (4.79)	7.33 (2.23)	6.90 (2.10)	190	50 (80)
Spartan MILAN	UK	16.18 (4,93)	7.36 (2.24)	7.93 (2.26)	190	50 (80)
Striker	UK	15.84 (4.83)	7.36 (2.24)	7.25 (2.21)	190	50 (80)
SU-100	USSR (Egypt, Syria)	31.00 (9.45)	9.85 (3.00)	7.38 (2.25)	500	30 (48)
Sucuri	Brazil	20.74 (6.32)	8.17 (2.49)	9.19 (2.80)	300	68 (110)

*Note that only armour piercing rounds are included.

LIGHT AFVs

Range miles (km)	Main armament cal. (mm)	Ammunition type(s)
250 (400)	90	HEAT, HESH
300 (384)	(25)	TOW
242 (390)	155	HE, nuclear, Copperhead
373 (600)	152	Shillelagh, HEAT
300 (483)	—	TOW
325 (520)	(20)	MILAN
250 (400)	155	HEAT
155 (250)	76	APHE, HEAT, HVAP
590 (950)	90	HEAT, APFSDS
400 (644)	76	HESH
300 (483)	—	MILAN
300 (483)	—	Swingfire
200 (320)	100	AP, APHE
372 (600)	105	APFSDS, HEAT

ducks and suffered heavy casualties. Soviet doctrine now demands that infantry de-bus when going into combat and precede their vehicles, but other nationalities have continued to develop MICVs from which infantry can fight rather than just being carried as passengers. There is further argument as to whether MICVs and APCs should be given an anti-tank capability as a matter of course or whether this should be left to helicopters, tanks and other dedicated delivery systems.

Hi-tech SPG

There is more agreement over self-propelled artillery since it is today widely recognised that crew protection against NBC contamination and smallarms fire is needed and that the smallest-calibre weapon capable of hurting modern tanks with HE is 150mm. This has led to the French 155mm GCT based on the AMX-30 chassis, to the Italian Palmaria based on the OT-40, and to the long-suffering NATO SP-70 project jointly shared by Britain, Italy, and West Germany. If, or when, SP-70 ever enters service, it will have a number of remarkable features. The gun itself is basically the FH-70 which is already in service as a towed piece. A collaborative venture between RARDE, Vickers Armstrong, Rheinmetall, and OTO-Melara, it is a superior 155mm gun/howitzer with a muzzle velocity of 2,714ft/s (827m/s), capable of firing all NATO standard rounds, and is thus compatible with the M109A2 down to its ability to fire Copperhead. Maximum range is said to be some 18 miles (30km). The SP-70's chassis is essentially that of the Leopard MBT. An important feature is an auto-reloader, enabling its ammunition supply to be replenished from outside without exposing the gun's crew to radiation or other hazards. Despite the many development problems, the British and German Armies at least are determined to acquire the SP-70.

Left: Rear view of a Soviet PT-76 light amphibious tank used by the US Army for training purposes. Note multiple hand-holds for infantry.

TANK BUSTERS

2S1 & 2S3

These two vehicles are the Soviet equivalent of the Western M109 and are grouped together for convenience even though they are really totally different other than both mounting a howitzer in a fully rotating turret. The 2S1 was first seen by Western observers in 1974 and mounts a 122mm D-30 howitzer with a muzzle velocity of 2,625ft/s (800m/s) on a modified PT-76 chassis with normal Soviet Christie-type torsion bar suspension. Like the latter, it is fully amphibious. The 2S3, which first appeared in 1973, shares the same chassis as the AFV introduced in 1964 that carries two SA-4 Ganef SAMs, and is consequently 4.9 tons heavier than the 19.7-ton 2S1. This vehicle mounts the 152mm D-20 howitzer which has a muzzle velocity of 2,150 ft/s (655m/s). Both the 2S1 and

Above: The 2S3 closely resembles the M109.

AML-90/Eland 90

The venerable four-wheeled AML-90 armoured car first went into production in France in 1960, since when over 3,000 have been built and many of them widely exported. A prime user has for many years been South Africa — the vehicles being licence-built under the designation Eland 90 — whose army has found the HEAT round effective against the T-54/55s of neighbouring hostile African nations. As a result Eland 90 is the prime equipment of all the South African Army's armoured car regiments despite its age. In recent years the French have developed an APFSDS round with a muzzle velocity of 4,430ft/s (1,350m/s) for the 90mm smoothbore gun, but it is not known whether South African Elands have been modified to accept this. A different double-baffle muzzle brake is necessary to absorb the extra recoil.

It is a simple but sturdily built box-like vehicle with armour plate up to 0.5in (12mm) thick giving adequate protection against smallarms fire. Weighing only 5.4 tons it has a good power-to-weight ratio of over 16bhp/ton despite its relatively small Panhard petrol engine, and has excellent cross-country mobility, being able to tackle slopes of up to 60 degrees. Due to a new low recoil system introduced by the South Africans, the gun can be fired in all directions from the fully traversing turret while the vehicle is on the move without any risk of being pushed over. Although not fully amphibious, the Eland can be fitted with flotation gear and propellers driven from the engine which give it a speed of some 4mph (6km/h). It has a crew of three, two in the turret, and an excellent reputation for robustness and reliability.

The Eland's turret has also been fitted to the South African Ratel 90 APC, which has a crew of four plus six infantrymen, giving this too an anti-tank capability.

LIGHT AFVs

2S3 were designed to replace earlier towed artillery pieces of the same calibres, and three batteries are issued to each front-line armoured regiment.

Crewed by four men, both vehicles carry 40 rounds of ammunition which in the case of the 2S1 includes a spin-stabilised HEAT round capable of penetrating 18in (460mm) at 1,100yd (1,000m), and in the case of the 2S3 both an armour-piercing high-explosive round (APHE) which will penetrate 5in (130mm) at the same range and a 2kT tactical nuclear shell, so although they are lightly armoured they both have excellent anti-tank capabilities. Rate of fire for the 2S1 is approximately five rounds per minute and that of the 2S3 probably slightly less. The 2S1's frontally mounted diesel engine gives a power-to-weight ratio of 12.2bhp/ton and the 2S3's 11.9, so neither vehicle is particularly mobile, although special extra-wide tracks can be fitted to the former to improve cross-country performance.

Above: 2S1s deployed in the indirect fire role.

Above: The rugged construction of the AML-90, seen here in French Army colours, has won it many export orders.

TANK BUSTERS

AMX-13

One of the most widely used tank-destroyers in the world, although officially designated an air-portable light tank, the 14.76-ton AMX-13 entered production in 1951, and is still in service with over 20 countries, including Israel. Weight was the prime consideration in its design but although armour protection is therefore necessarily low (at a maximum 1.5in/40mm) it has always enjoyed excellent mobility and has been progressively modernised and up-gunned to meet changing battlefield requirements. The petrol engine is at the front and the fuel tanks at the rear for increased protection and for a tank of its age it has a high power-to-weight ratio of 18bhp/ton. It was the first production tank in the world to have an automatic loader, reducing the size of the turret and requiring a crew of only three. The gun is rigidly mounted in the turret which oscillates independently of the hull to keep the gun in track, and a high rate of fire of up to 12 rounds per minute can be achieved; however, once the 12 rounds in the twin-carousel auto-loader have been fired, they can only be reloaded from outside the vehicle, posing an obvious battlefield hazard for the crew. A total of 34 rounds of 90mm ammunition is carried, predominantly a HEAT round with a muzzle velocity of 3,118ft/s (950m/s) and the ability to penetrate armour up to 12½in (320mm) thick. In addition to the original 75mm or more recent 90 or 105mm guns which can be fitted, up to four SS-12 or, more recently, HOT

ASU-85

Introduced in 1961 to supplement and eventually replace the earlier ASU-57, the ASU-85 is an air-portable tank-destroyer designed to give mobile anti-tank support to Soviet airborne troops, nine vehicles being assigned to each regiment, and can itself be parachute-dropped. It is based upon the chassis of the PT-76 light tank but lacks the latter's amphibious quality. A low, well-sloped superstructure with armour up to 1.5in (40mm) thick contains the crew of four, and the 85mm L/53 M1944 gun for which 40 rounds of APHE are carried. This weapon has a muzzle velocity of 2,600ft/s (800m/s), an effective range of up to 2,200yd (2,000m) in the anti-tank role and a rate of fire of four rounds per minute. Although the gun is old it is obviously capable of destroying MBTs below the calibre of Abrams, Challenger, and Leopard 2.

LIGHT AFVs

ATGWs or their equivalent can be mounted on the front of the turret.

While the AMX-13 has not been an unqualified battlefield success either in Indochina or the Middle East, its low silhouette and high mobility still make it a versatile anti-tank vehicle nearly 40 years after it first went into service. Numerous variants, including anti-aircraft, bridgelayer, engineer, and 155mm howitzer versions have also been produced.

Above: A wire-guided SS-11 first-generation anti-tank missile is launched from an AMX-13.

The ASU-85 is powered by a rear-mounted diesel engine giving a power-to-weight ratio of 17.4bhp/ton which provides reasonable cross-country mobility, while in common with other Soviet AFVs extra fuel tanks can be strapped on to the vehicle's rear. (These are obviously discarded in combat.) The vehicle has an IR searchlight mounted co-axially on the gun mantlet, and it is probable that passive light vision sights are also fitted nowadays. There is a co-axial 7.62mm machine-gun and full NBC filtration.

Although the ASU-85 is outdated by modern standards it does provide Soviet airborne troops with an anti-tank capability lacked by Western forces, and will probably continue in service for some time.

Below: ASU-85s of the Chernigov Red Banner Division disembark from their AN-12 'Cub' transports to support parachute troops during a winter exercise near the River Dvina.

TANK BUSTERS

BRDM-2

Originally designed as a light four-wheeled scout car to replace the earlier BTR-40 in the reconnaissance role while the BTR-60 replaced it as a troop carrier, the BRDM-1 and -2 has emerged subsequently as a light, fast, dedicated tank-destroyer of lethal capabilities. First generation BRDMs were equipped with three AT-1 Snapper wire-guided ATGW firing rails, then with four AT-2 Swatter radio-guided rails, and finally with six AT-3 Saggers. In the first two instances the roof hatches had to be opened to enable the launchers to be raised but in the last the whole roof elevated as a unit (rather like the British Striker), saving time and giving the four-man crew a little extra protection.

In the BRDM-2 a number of changes were made, noticeably increasing the engine's performance and moving it to the rear of the hull, and adding a small 14.5mm machine-gun turret to the top of the crew compartment at the front. Although the vehicle's overall weight increased from 5.5 to 6.9 tons, the new engine gave an improved power-to-weight ratio of 20.3bhp/ton with considerably enhanced overall speed and mobility. An unusual feature of the BRDM is the four small belly wheels which can be lowered to reduce ground pressure in mud or snow. The BRDM-2 has rails for six AT-3s or more recently AT-5 Spandrels or AT-6 Saggers, with stowage for up to 14 missiles.

Although very lightly armoured, and festooned with hatches and other appurtenances which ruin its ballistic deflection abilities, the BRDM-2's combination of speed and state-of-the-art missiles make it a formidable opponent and one which is likely to be in the forefront of any Soviet offensive in Western Europe. It is also built under licence in Hungary and in Czechoslovakia as the FUG with an 81mm recoilless gun.

Right: BRDM-2 crews pose for the camera. The six AT-3 Sagger missiles retract into the hull when not in use.

Commando

One of the most widely used vehicles in the US Army, the Cadillac-Gage Commando armoured car entered production in 1964. It has subsequently been produced in four different versions, saw extensive service in Vietnam, and has been exported or licence-built in 20 other countries. Early models had four wheels but the latest variant, the V-300, has six, all versions being fully amphibious, using their large cleated tyres for propulsion. Four-wheel versions have a conventional layout but in the V-300 the engine is at the front for extra protection. The Commando is a tall, bulky vehicle with a crew of either two or three, and is primarily used in the reconnaissance and convoy protection roles. It has well-sloped welded steel armour resistant to smallarms fire and in the anti-tank role is fitted with a Belgian Cockerill 90mm gun. (In the earlier four-wheeled versions it was impossible to fire this except from a stationary position on flat ground without running the risk of overturning the vehicle due to the recoil!) This hi-tech gun has no fewer than 60 rifling grooves, which reduces erosion and gives a barrel life of at least 2,000 rounds, while the 20ft (6.09m) pitch enables it to fire HEAT rounds without the usual problem of spin destabilisation ruining their effectiveness and accuracy. A three-baffle muzzle-brake reduces the recoil force sufficiently to enable the gun to be fired on the move, making the Commando a highly effective tankbuster, and its high mobility makes it a difficult target.

In 1978 Cadillac-Gage introduced a new variant designated Commando Scout, which reverts to the four-wheel, two-man layout but with the engine at the front and with vastly improved armour layout. This is usually equipped with TOW missiles in the anti-tank role although 20mm and 30mm cannons or a 106mm recoilless gun are alternative options. The Scout is both lower and faster than the V-300 and a significant improvement over all earlier armoured cars.

Right: A factory-fresh Cadillac-Gage Commando.

LIGHT AFVs

TANK BUSTERS

FV102 Striker

Striker is one of a series of light Combat Vehicles Reconnaissance (Tracked) (CVRT) developed by the FVRDE at Chobham during the 1960s and '70s, popularly known as the Scorpion family. All vehicles in the series share the same basic aluminium-armoured hull and suspension, with minor differences in wheelbase and wheel spacing, are powered by the famous Jaguar 4.2-litre sports car engine, and are designed to operate in the front line in the tactical reconnaissance role. Although both Scorpion, with its 76mm gun, and Scimitar, with its quick-firing 30mm Rarden cannon, have a limited anti-tank role against the sides and rear of Soviet MBTs, Striker is the dedicated tankbuster of the series.

In overall shape it bears a striking resemblance to Spartan, which is the troop-carrying model, but instead of infantry it carries ten Swingfire ATGWs, five internally and five in an elevating launcher at the vehicle's rear. This deceptive

LIGHT AFVs

similarity between the two vehicles is quite deliberate, and designed to keep enemy tank crews guessing until a missile is on its way. Being wire-guided, Swingfire is not an easy missile to control; after launch, it automatically reduces altitude to bring it within the operator's sight at around 150yd (140m) and then has to be manually guided by means of a 'joy-stick' to its target up to 4,375yd (4,000m) away. To protect its crew from retaliatory fire, a remote-control firing post can be situated up to 110yd (100m) from the vehicle itself.

Striker is only lightly armoured, although its front-mounted engine confers a degree of extra protection, but it has excellent mobility, with a power-to-weight ratio of 23bhp/ton, and full NBC protection for its crew of three. It is a potent weapon on the modern battlefield and considerably cheaper than Chieftain or Challenger.

Below: A Swingfire missile at the moment of launch from the raised bin on the rear hull of an FV102. Today this is the British Army's dedicated anti-tank weapons system.

TANK BUSTERS

Jagdpanzer Kanone

During World War II the Germans became expert at designing a wide range of tank-destroyers mounting a powerful gun with limited traverse in a low and well-sloped superstructure, culminating in the famous Jagdpanther. Following the Federal Republic's admission to NATO, in the late 1950s Rheinstall Sonderfertigung of Kassel commenced work on a new Jagdpanzer, over 800 of which were eventually produced for Germany and Belgium. Bearing a striking resemblance to wartime designs with its highly sloped glacis up to 2in (50mm) thick, low, flat roof and prominent, curved mantlet for its main 90mm Rheinmetall gun, it has a crew of four and stowage space for 51 rounds of ammunition. Comprising either HEAT or HESH, these have an effective range of 2,200yd (2,000m) and the vehicle has a high rate of fire of up to 12 rounds per minute. A white light/IR searchlight is mounted above the gun and traverses with it, while a laser rangefinder has been introduced in a recent modernisation refit. Further refinements include improved fire-control systems, NBC protection and better fire-fighting equipment.

The Jagpanzer Kanone's Daimler-Benz diesel engine gives it a power-to-weight ratio of 19.4bhp/ton with excellent mobility, and its gun has a traverse of 15 degrees either side of its centreline. These are excellent fighting qualities for the largely defensive battle NATO expects to fight in Europe should it ever come to an armed confrontation with the Soviet Union.

Although production has ceased and an SS-11 missile-armed version designated Racketenjagdpanzer has been abandoned in favour of the Marder MILAN, Jagdpanzer Kanone remains a formidable tankbuster.

Right: The 90mm gun-armed Jagdpanzer Kanone tank-destroyer on manoeuvres with the West German Army.

M2/M3 Bradley

Although the US Army has long had a reliable, though large and bulky, APC in the form of the M113, neither this nor the disastrous M551 Sheridan light tank which first entered production in 1962 offered the qualities required for an MICV on the battlefield of the 1980s. At the same time the Army also needed a new reconnaissance vehicle, so in the late 1960s six companies were invited to tender, to very exacting standards, to fulfil both requirements. From this, in 1972, emerged the first four prototypes of the FMC IFV XM2 and CFV XM3 which eventually went into production in 1978 as the (infantry) M2 and (cavalry) M3 Bradley. The main difference between the two vehicles is that the former is designed to carry a three-man crew and up to six infantry, while the latter just has two infantrymen to conduct reconnaissances on foot. The M3 also has increased ammunition stowage space for both the Hughes 25mm Chain Gun and the two TOW launchers either side of the turret. In addition, the M2 has smallarms firing ports for its infantry complement while the M3 does not.

Both vehicles are complex and expensive, featuring a mixture of aluminium and laminate armour capable, it is claimed, of withstanding high velocity AP rounds up to 23mm calibre; however, aluminium armour vaporises when struck by a HEAT round. Nevertheless, the Chain Gun (for which 300 or 900 rounds are carried depending on variant) gives excellent results against other light AFVs, and the TOW missiles give similar performance against MBTs. Five TOW rounds are carried internally by the M2 and ten by the M3.

As befits their battlefield role, particularly in Europe with its many rivers, both M2 and M3 are fully amphibious, being driven by their tracks. However, the Detroit Diesel engine gives only a disappointing power-to-weight ratio of 13bhp/ton.

Right: An M2 Bradley infantry combat vehicle during an exercise with the US Army 2nd Armoured Division in Texas.

LIGHT AFVs

TANK BUSTERS

M109A1/M109A2

In 1953 the US Army began development of a new 110mm howitzer to replace its current 105mm models and when the M113 APC entered service in 1960 trials were conducted mounting this gun in a fully rotating turret on a stretched M113 chassis. Eventually the 110mm howitzer was dropped and the turret modified to take a 155mm howitzer instead, and this entered production in 1963 as the M109. Since then it has become the most important SPG in US service and has been widely exported, over 3,700 having been manufactured. The wisdom of opting for a 155mm weapon has been proven in the Middle East where in 1967 and again in 1973 the Israelis found that artillery of 105mm calibre was inadequate to break up mass tank attacks. The basic M109 concept has since been adopted by France in the GCT, by Italy in the Palmaria, and by Sweden in the VK-155, as well as by Britain, Italy and West Germany in the long-drawn-out SP70 project.

The basic M109 and its successors, M109A1 and M109A2 (which have different versions of the M185 155mm howitzer) are unusual in having all-round aluminium armour protection up to 0.75in (20mm) thick and a tank-type turret rather than the more usual limited traverse weapon. Both features obviously enhance their survivability and give them superior anti-armour potential in support of MBTs. The gun in the M109A1, for which 28 rounds are carried in the turret, has a range of 19,700yd (18,000m), and can fire tactical nuclear shells as well as conventional HE rounds. The latter will not destroy a modern MBT except by sheer luck, but will severely disable one and certainly concuss the crew. The M109A2 can also fire the Martin Marietta Copperhead laser-guided 'smart' shell which is a dedicated anti-tank projectile, the target being marked by a laser in an aircraft or from a ground position and the Copperhead homing in on the reflected radiation. Although Copperhead can be fired accurately onto a marked

Right: This camouflaged M109A2 displays the imposing length of its 155mm gun, complete with large muzzle brake and fume extractor.

Below: A whitewash-camouflaged M109 with its barrel lowered as it would be when used in the anti-tank role.

LIGHT AFVs

target up to 10 miles (16km) away, due to the cost of developing it and the price of individual rounds, production ceased in 1982 and the 8,000-plus rounds manufactured have been issued solely to the US Rapid Deployment Force. It is likely, despite all official denials, that an enhanced radiation (i.e. neutron) shell has or is being developed which will further increase the M109's effectiveness against large tank formations. For stability when firing, the M109 has two hydraulically-operated recoil spades at its rear.

The M109 has a crew of six and is powered by a reliable front-mounted turbocharged Detroit Diesel. The vehicle's low weight of 24.55 tons gives a comparatively good power-to-weight ratio of 18bhp/ton. It also has a limited swimming ability using its tracks for propulsion after buoyancy bags have been attached. A 0.5in (12.7mm) machine-gun is provided for local self-defence, and the M109 also has full NBC and fire-fighting equipment.

The M109 forms the main component of American and British medium artillery regiments in Europe and will continue to play an important role as an armoured support vehicle into the 1990s.

TANK BUSTERS

Marder MILAN

With their wide experience of APCs from the war, a new vehicle was an obvious priority for the reconstituted Bundeswehr in the late 1950s. However, the introduction of Marder, as the Rheinstall Sonderfertigung vehicle eventually became known, was delayed for a considerable length of time because the German Army insisted upon a vehicle which could not just carry troops into battle, but from which they could fight if necessary. This meant some form of gun in a fully rotating turret as well as firing ports for the six-man infantry squad in the vehicle's rear, and a roofed superstructure with NBC protection. Hatches in the roof to the rear of the turret also enable the infantry to operate in the open, a particularly useful attribute during urban street fighting. The infantry 'debus' via a power-operated hatch in the vehicle's rear. All of these features, coupled with the need for high mobility and frontal armour which would give protection

LIGHT AFVs

against weapons up to 20mm in calibre, caused many delays and the first production batch was not completed until the end of 1970, the vehicle entering service the following year.

It has a low two-man turret with a main Rheinmetall quick-firing 20mm cannon for which 1,250 rounds are carried, a 7.62mm machine-gun which can be fired independently from within the vehicle, and, to make it an effective tank-destroyer as well, a MILAN ATGW launcher. Many other NATO APCs are being similarly fitted, so Marder is here taken as representative.

Marder's Mercedes-Benz diesel engine, fitted in the well-sloped hull front for extra protection, gives a power-to-weight ratio of 21.6bhp/ton with excellent cross-country performance, while its low silhouette further enhances its battlefield survivability.

Below: The commander of a Marder aims the turret-mounted MILAN which gives this APC a useful anti-tank capability.

Guns, Artillery, Artillery Rockets

THE CONVENTIONAL anti-tank gun which played such a vital role in World War II is, today, virtually defunct. There are a few exceptions: the Soviet 57mm M1943, 85mm D-44, and 100mm T-12, the Belgian and Swiss 90mm Mecar, PaK 50 and 57, and no doubt a variety of otherwise obsolete weapons still held in the arsenals of small Third World countries. The Soviet Union has always been artillery-orientated and has had a high proportion of field guns of all calibres in comparison with other nations — usually dual-purpose (i.e. capable of firing AP as well as HE rounds) — and significantly still keeps in operational use weapons of almost 50 years' vintage. The main disadvantage of the conventional rifled anti-tank gun is that, in order to fire a high-velocity round of sufficient weight (and therefore kinetic energy) to defeat the armour thicknesses of post-war MBTs, it has to be quite large, heavy to move, and difficult to conceal, as well as usually requiring a crew of several men.

Field artillery

The 57mm M1943 is now obsolete but the 85mm D-44 and 100mm T-12 are in widespread use throughout the Warsaw Pact and elsewhere. The former is unusual in being able to be fitted with a small auxiliary motor (when it is designated SD-44), allowing it to be driven around the battlefield under its own power — an idea adopted in the British/West German/Italian FH70. The T-12 is a smoothbore weapon which has largely replaced the older M1955 and fires fin-stabilised rounds. In general appearance both are very similar to World War II guns, with split trails and splinter shields. The Mecar is a lightweight weapon which has been exported to several countries although it is not in use within NATO. It is particularly useful against fixed strongpoints since its HEAT round can penetrate nearly 4ft (1,200mm) of reinforced concrete. The PaK 50 and 57 guns are no longer in production but are still in service with Swiss infantry battalions. Each of the above requires a crew of between four and six men.

The problems of size and lack of mobility with conventional anti-tank guns were appreciated during World War II and led to the design and manufacture of a wide variety of recoilless guns of all calibres, pioneered by the Germans for airborne use. These are light, since barrel stresses are low, and only require similarly light mountings, which can be easily moved around the battlefield by manpower or can be fitted to small vehicles such as Jeeps and scout cars. The big disadvantage of a recoilless gun has always been that in order to balance the recoil of the propellant charge an equal charge has to be fired simultaneously backwards, which is both hazardous to any unwary infantry in the vicinity and gives away the gun position to the enemy. For that reason, although there are an enormous variety of recoilless guns still in service around the world — and, indeed, still under development — they are mainly today of the smaller, infantry-portable, one-shot disposable variety like the Swedish Miniman.

Nevertheless, larger weapons such as the US 106mm M40 are still potent tankbusters under the right conditions, and both the Chinese and the Finns, with their multiple-calibre Raikka system, continue to develop new guns of larger calibre. A recent development which overcomes the problem of backblast and exposure is the experimental West German Armbrust. This light (13lb/6kg) infantry weapon contains an explosive charge in its centre in between two pistons. The HEAT projectile, which is said to have an effective range of 330yd (300m), is loaded at one end while the other is filled with a counterweight of plastic

Conventional artillery, whether self-propelled or towed, is still a potent anti-tank weapon, and new, more powerful types of ammunition, especially for artillery rockets, are under development.

flakes. When fired, the explosive drives both pistons outwards, hurling the projectile at its target and the plastic flakes harmlessly out of the rear. The pistons lock at each end of the barrel so no smoke or flame emerges, while the sound of the discharge is reduced to a muffled thump.

Recoilless guns

One of the most common man-portable recoilless guns in existence today is the Swedish 84mm Carl Gustav, which can engage moving targets at up to 440yd (400m) and stationary ones at 600yd (550m). Because it is heavy (31lb/14.2kg) it is normally operated by two men, one carrying the launcher and a couple of 5.7lb (2.6kg) HEAT rounds and the other a number of further rounds. Unlike most earlier recoilless guns which had wheeled carriages, the Carl Gustav is designed to be fired from over the shoulder, and for a weapon of its calibre has an impressive anti-armour capability — hence its wide adoption around the world. Designated a Medium Anti-armour Weapon (MAW), the Carl Gustav seems likely to be replaced eventually with smaller and lighter 'one-shot' disposable Light Anti-armour Weapons (LAWs) such as Miniman — another Swedish FFV Ordnance product. The full weight of a loaded Miniman, whose armour penetration capability is almost as good as that of the Carl Gustav (albeit at reduced range), is only 6.4lb (2.9kg) since it is constructed of glass-reinforced plastic; and since it is only 35.4in (900mm) in length it is a weapon that every infantryman can carry in addition to his other equipment. It is simple to use without any training or experience — indeed, complete instructions are painted on the barrel! Although heavier, at 13.2lb (6kg), the FFV AT-4 of 84mm calibre promises even better results, and it is likely that other recoilless weapons of this nature will emerge since they are generally lighter and cheaper than ATGWs.

The replacement, by and large, of the conventional, large recoilless gun such as the M40 or Wombat is nevertheless the ATGW, which can frequently be fired by remote control so that the gunner's position remains concealed. Not needing barrels or, these days, cumbersome launchers, ATGWs have greater range and armour-penetrating ability per pound or kilo of hardware to be lugged around the battlefield than any gun so far devised. Moreover, in the fast-moving and fluid European battlefield conceived by tacticians of both East and West, mobility is a paramount factor.

Ordinary gun/howitzers, normally of 105mm calibre and above, are not designed principally as anti-tank weapons to be fired over open sights, but a variety of HESH, spin- or fin-stablised HEAT, and APHE rounds have been developed for ▶

Below: The US 155mm M198, which fires HEAT rounds out to 24,060 yd (22,000m).

TANK BUSTERS

Guns, Artillery, Artillery Rockets

Calibre (mm)	Name	Origin	Muzzle velocity fps (m/s)	Effective AT range yd (m)	Ammunition type(s)	Rate of fire (rpm)	Armour penetr. in (mm)
41	Raikka (rec.)	Finland	558 (170)	220 (200)	HEAT	n/a	n/a
51	Field Rocket System	Italy	n/a	n/a	AT-AP	48 (salvo)	n/a
55	Raikka (rec.)	Finland	558 (170)	220 (200)	HEAT	n/a	n/a
55	M-55 (rec.)	Finland	n/a	220 (200)	HEAT	3-5	7.9 (200)
57	M-43	USSR	2,300-4,170 (700-1,270)	550 (500)	AP, APHE, HVAP	4	4 (100)
57	Type 36 (rec.)	China	n/a	490 (450)	HEAT	n/a	2.5 (63.5)
68	SARPAC (rec.)	France	302-492 (92-150)	220-711 (200-650)	HEAT, APHE	n/a	11.8+ (300+)
70	RADIRS Multiple Rocket System	USA	n/a	766-16,410+ (700-15,000+)	AT	7-19 tubes x2-6 (salvo)	n/a
73	SPG-9	USSR	1,428 (435)	1,422 (1,300)	HEAT	n/a	15+ (390+)
74	Miniman (disp.)	Sweden	525 (160)	273 (250)	HEAT	1	13.4 (340)
75	Type 52 (rec.)	China	n/a	875 (800)	HEAT	n/a	9 (228)
81	Merlin	UK	Under development, no data available				
81	Raikka (rec.)	Finland	820-3,280 (250-1,000)	440+ (400+)	HEAT	n/a	n/a
82	B-10 (rec.)	USSR	1,050 (320)	440 (400)	HEAT	6	9.5 (240)
82	M59 (rec.)	Czechoslovakia	n/a	1,313 (1,200)	HEAT	n/a	9.8 (250)
82	M60 (rec.)	Yugoslavia	1,250 (380)	1,640 (1,500)	HEAT	n/a	8.66 (220)
82	T-21 (rec.)	Czechoslovakia	876 (267)	500 (457)	HEAT	n/a	9 (228)
82	Type 65 (rec.)	China	1,050 (320)	427 (390)	HEAT	6-7	9.45 (240)
84	AT4 (disp.)	Sweden	952 (290)	328 (300)	HEAT	1	17.7+ (450+)
84	M2/M3 Carl Gustav (rec.)	Sweden	1,017 (310)	490 (450)	AT	6	15.75 (400)
85	D-44	USSR	2,600-3,380 (792-1,030)	1,750 (1,600)	APHE, HVAP	15	5.12 (130)
90	M67 (rec.)	USA	n/a	440 (400)	HEAT	5	n/a
90	Mecar	Belgium	2,077 (633)	1,100 (1,000)	HEAT	n/a	13.78 (350)
90	PV-1110 (rec.)	Sweden	2,133 (650)	985 (900)	HEAT	6	21.6 (550)
90	Pak 50/57	Switzerland	n/a	656-875 (600-800)	HEAT	20	n/a

GUNS, ARTILLERY, ARTILLERY ROCKETS

Calibre (mm)	Name	Origin	Muzzle velocity fps (m/s)	Effective AT range yd (m)	Ammunition type(s)	Rate of fire (rpm)	Armour penetr. in (mm)
90	Type 51 (rec.)	China	325 (99)	1,313 (1,200)	HEAT	n/a	10.5 (267)
95	SM58-61 (rec.)	Finland	2,018 (615)	1,100 (1,000)	HEAT	6-8	11.8 (300)
100	T-12	USSR	3,280 (1,000)	2,000 (1,250)	APHE, HEAT	7-8	7.1 (180)
105	L13A1	UK	2,324 (708)	18,817 (17,200)	HESH	12	n/a
105	L118	UK	2,324 (708)	875 (800)	HESH	6	n/a
105	M27 (rec)	USA	1,250 (381)	1,100 (1,000)	HEAT	n/a	n/a
105	M102	USA	2,000 (610)	12,575 (11,500)	HEAT	n/a	n/a
105	M65 (rec.)	Yugoslavia	1,640 (500)	656 (600)	HEAT	6	13 (330)
105	M1968 (rec.)	Argentina	1,313 (400)	1,313 (1,200)	ECH	3-5	7.9 (200)
105	Type 75 (rec.)	China	1,650 (503)	635 (580)	HEAT	5-6	5.9 (150)
106	M40 (rec.)	USA	1,660 (506)	1,200 (1,100)	HEAT	5	n/a
107	B-11 (rec.)	USSR	n/a	490 (450)	HEAT	6	15 (380)
110	Light Artillery Rocket System	W. Germany	n/a	7,111-1-6,410 (6,500--15,000)	APHE	36 (salvo)	n/a
120	Raikka (rec.)	Finland	2,950-4,920 (900-1,500)	1,640 (1,500)	HVAPDS	n/a	n/a
120	Wombat (rec.)	UK	1,520 (463)	1,200 (1,100)	HESH	4	n/a
122	BM-21 Rocket System	USSR	2,295 (699)	16,395+ (15,000+)	HE	40 (salvo)	n/a
122	D-30	USSR	2,265 (690)	3,830 (3,500)	HEAT	4-5	18 (460)
122	Field Rocket System	Italy	n/a	8,750-36,100 (8,000-33,000)	AT	40 (salvo)	n/a
130	M-46	USSR	3,050 (930)	1,090 (1,000)	APHE	4-5	9 (230)
140	BM-14-17 Rocket System	USSR	1,320 (402)	10,730 (9,810)	HE	17 (salvo)	n/a
140	Multiple Rocket System	Spain	2,255 (687)	30,630 (28,000)	AP	40 (salvo)	3.94 (100)
152	D-20	USSR	2,150 (655)	1,090 (1,000)	APHE	4	5 (130)
155	M114A2	USA	1,850 (564)	21,125 (19,315)	HEAT	n/a	n/a
155	M185	USA	2,245 (684)	19,690 (18,000)	HEAT	2-3	n/a

Table continued on next page

TANK BUSTERS

Table continued from previous page

Calibre (mm)	Name	Origin	Muzzle velocity fps (m/s)	Effective AT range yd (m)	Ammunition type(s)	Rate of fire (rpm)	Armour penetr. in (mm)
155	M198	USA	n/a	24,060 (22,000)	HEAT	n/a	n/a
160	Light Artillery Rocket System	Israel	n/a	32,820 (30,000)	AP	18 (salvo)	n/a
175	M113	USA	3,000 (914)	35,770 (32,700)	HE	1-2	n/a
180	S-23	USSR	2,600 (790)	33,245 (30,400)	HE, nuclear	1	n/a
203	M201	USA	2,333 (711)	23,300 (21,300)	HE, nuclear	0.5	n/a
220	BM-27 Rocket System	USSR	n/a	43,760 (40,000)	HE	16 (salvo)	n/a
227	Multiple Launch Rocket System	USA	Supersonic	32,820 (30,000)	AP, SADA-RM(?)	12 (salvo)	4+ (100+)
240	BM-24 Rocket System	USSR	1,190 (363)	11,268 (10,300)	HE	12 (salvo)	n/a
250	BM-25 Rocket System	USSR	n/a	61,155 (55,900)	HE	6 (salvo)	n/a

(rec. = recoilless; disp. = disposable)

▶ most weapons. With indirect fire, using HE, conventional artillery is relatively useless, it being estimated that some 2,500 rounds have to be fired to disable a single tank, on average. More recent developments with smart projectiles such as Copperhead and SADARM make conventional artillery pieces more useful in the anti-tank role, but such munitions are very expensive and it remains to be seen how prevalent they become. Certainly the towed artillery piece is rapidly becoming a thing of the past (except, again, in Russia and Soviet client states), as is the open-topped SPG such as the M107 or M110, with an ever-increasing emphasis on at least a degree of all-round armour protection.

The Soviet Union has also been a pioneer of the free-flight unguided artillery rocket, and over the years Russian designers have produced a wide variety of multi-barrel projectors of various calibres, usually mounted on trucks. These enable a field commander to lay down a rapid and concentrated barrage of HE, chemical agents or submunitions such as mines, while larger rockets can also have nuclear warheads. It is only comparatively recently (since the early 1970s) that Western nations have come to appreciate the value of such systems, but this has now led to several new multiple-barrel projectors mounted on trucks or lightly armoured, tracked, vehicles. The most important of these to NATO is the Multiple Launch Rocket System (MLRS), but others include the Italian 51mm and 122mm Field Rocket Systems, the privately developed American RADIRS 70mm system, the West German 110mm Light Artillery Rocket System, the Spanish 140mm Multiple Rocket System and the Israeli 160mm Light Artillery Rocket System. All of these are free-flight projectiles with ranges in excess of 9 miles (15km) and their warheads include anti-armour rounds or submunitions.

Smart shells

Many of the most significant developments of recent years have been in the field of smart artillery shells. SADARM is likely to prove the

GUNS, ARTILLERY, ARTILLERY ROCKETS

most significant of these for NATO, because, in addition to the six Skeet explosively forged projectiles (EFP) in the MLRS round, a smaller version with three submunitions to be fired from 155mm howitzers has also been developed independently in the United States, West Germany, and in Sweden; the Rheinmetall round carries the acronym ZEPL while the Bofors round is designated Bonus. In March 1986 the US Army issued a specification for a superior MLRS round with twice the range of the existing rocket, and Martin-Marietta, with their experience from the Copperhead programme, have been selected to design a new precision-guided top/bottom attack anti-armour submunition.

Another new American 155mm projectile is the Remote Anti-Armour Mine System (RAAMS), each round containing nine M718 or M741 anti-tank mines, which can be fired up to 10 miles (16km) into the path of a Soviet tank force. Similar developments are taking place in Germany where Rheinmetall are working on a 155mm anti-armour round designated EPHRAM. This will descend to a height of around 2,600ft (800m), whereupon a sensor will scan the ground below for tanks, and small side rockets will direct the hollow-charge projectile onto target. Another Rheinmetall shell designed for use with the FH70 is the RB63 which contains 63 HEAT bomblets; this will have a range of 24,500yd (22,400m). A smaller version, RB49 (with 49 submunitions), will have a range of 32,800yd (30,000m). Rheinmetall also have a projected SADARM-type round to be fired from the M110 8in (203mm) SPH.

New anti-armour rounds to be fired from mortars are also being developed in the UK and Sweden. The British bomb is of 81mm calibre to fit the standard 81mm mortar which is in use with some 40 countries. Called Merlin, it is a terminally guided HEAT round. The Swedish design, called Strix, is basically the same but designed for use with 120mm mortars. It will have an IR sensor and HEAT warhead while a sustainer rocket motor will also be made available to extend its range.

Top-attack weapons

It will be noted that all recent developments in anti-tank artillery are designed to attack their targets from above or below, where they are most vulnerable. Reactive armour will confer some protection against such HEAT rounds, for minimal weight penalty, but will be ineffective against EFPs. Moreover, in order to beat reactive armour, experimental rounds of double HEAT are being tested. So the endless competition between tank and gun designers continues.

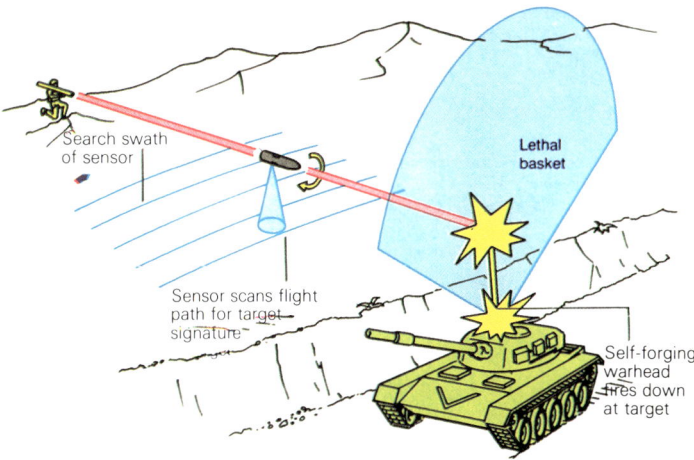

Above: The Smart Top Attack Fire and Forget (STAFF) system fired by tanks, artillery or rocket launchers. The projectile and sensor spin in flight, searching for a target to attack from above.

TANK BUSTERS

106mm M40/A1/A2/A4 Recoilless Rifle

The best-known, most successful and widely used recoilless anti-tank gun in the world — even today — dates back to 1943 when the Infantry Section of the US Research and Development Service began to investigate anew the abandoned principle of Cleland Davis's original recoilless gun of 1914. The principle is simplicity itself — for every action there is an equal and opposite reaction. In a normal gun this expresses itself as recoil. If, however, a barrel is open at both ends and a force equal to that of the projectile propellant is fired from one end while the projectile is launched from the other, there is no recoil. In the early days it was hoped that this principle could be used to mount large-calibre guns on aircraft, but this proved unworkable, and the idea was only revived in order to give the infantry a lighter and therefore more mobile anti-tank weapon than the guns then in service, one which could even be mounted on a vehicle as small as a Jeep. The Infantry Section tests resulted in recoilless guns of 57, 75 and

GUNS, ARTILLERY, ARTILLERY ROCKETS

105mm calibre entering service late in World War II. After the war two further designs, the 90mm M67 and 105mm M27, were produced, but the latter was a clumsy and over-heavy weapon so it was redesigned and finally entered service in the mid-1950s as the M40. It is, actually, of 105mm calibre but was designated 106mm to prevent confusion with its ill-fated precursor.

The M40 is comparatively light at 462lb (209.5kg) and is normally mounted on a small three-wheeled tripod in its infantry variant, which can be manhandled by just two soldiers. It was the first weapon in the world to have a co-axial ranging machine-gun (0.5in) firing tracer, as well as a telescopic sight, the former being used when firing HEAT and the latter when firing HE or anti-personnel-tracer (APERS-T), maximum range being 8,424yd (7,700m). The rounds are plastic-bagged and perforated to allow the expanding gas to escape into the reaction chamber.

The M40 has been sold to or built under licence in 36 countries and has seen action in every major conflict around the world over the last 30 years.

Below: Men of the US 82nd Airborne Division with a Jeep-mounted 106mm M40. Note the ranging machine-gun on top of the barrel and elevating handwheel at the rear.

TANK BUSTERS

122mm D-30 Field Howitzer

One of the most important weapons in the Soviet armoury, issued in batteries of four throughout the Warsaw Pact as well as various Arab nations, the D-30 first appeared in 1963 as a replacement for the 122mm M1938. This was the standard Russian field howitzer throughout World War II and was of conventional design with a split trail carriage and splinter shield. Apart from an improved rifled barrel, with large muzzle brake, the main innovation on the D-30 is its three-legged platform, based on original Skoda designs for the German Army in 1943–44. When this is lowered (raising the wheels off the ground) the gun can be rapidly traversed to any point of the compass, a particularly valuable asset in a fast-moving battle, allowing the seven-man crew to switch targets very quickly.

The wheels' axle is at the gun's centre of gravity in this configuration, conferring extra stability, and the weapon is anchored by driving perforated steel spikes into the ground through the ends of the three legs. On the move, these legs are folded side-by-side under the barrel, the gun being towed by means of a large lug under the muzzle brake.

The D-30's barrel is trunnioned well back to give 65 degrees elevation in the indirect fire mode, and is surmounted by a large recoil system. There is a semi-automatic sliding block for the cased, variable-charge ammunition rounds, which weigh up to 48lb (21.8kg) and include a 31lb (14kg) fin-stabilised HEAT round for direct-fire anti-tank use. This proved highly effective against Israeli armour during the 1973 October War. The gun weighs 6,944lb (3,150kg) and its maximum range firing HE or chemical rounds is 16,370yd (15,300m). Line-of-sight firing is by optical telescope.

Right: The unusual 'tripod' platform of the D-30 gives the gun a low silhouette, essential in the anti-tank role.

BM-24, -25 & -27 Rocket Systems

The first two of the Soviet Army's closest equivalents to MLRS, BM-24 and -25, have both been in service since the late 1950s but remain highly potent battlefield support weapons and are in service with many countries despite the introduction of the more modern BM-27 in 1977. The BM-24 is still used by the East German Army but has been withdrawn from Russian service. The Soviet Union has always relied heavily on free-flight artillery rockets (as the Germans discovered when they encountered the Katyusha in 1941), and until very recently they have enjoyed considerable superiority over NATO forces in these types of weapon. Apart from the BM-24, -25 and -27, other systems include the smaller-calibre BM-21 and BM-14-7, but many are now obsolete even though still in service with client nations.

The BM-24 consists of 12 open-frame launchers with 140-degree traverse on ZIL-157 six-wheeled trucks or tube launchers on AT-S tractors. The 240mm rockets each weigh 248lb (112kg) yet the launchers can be reloaded in the remarkably short time of three to four minutes. The 250mm BM-25 is the largest-calibre artillery rocket in service anywhere in the world, with the greatest range, and the only one to be liquid-fuelled. The individual weapons weigh 1,000lb (455kg), six being loaded in launchers on KrAZ-214 trucks. Reloading time is unknown.

The latest in the range, the BM-27, is a 220mm rocket weighing 794lb (360kg), 16 being loaded on a ZIL-135 truck. Reloading time is 15-20 minutes. It is strange, incidentally, that the Soviets persist in mounting their artillery rockets

GUNS, ARTILLERY, ARTILLERY ROCKETS

on soft-skin vehicles when they have developed tracked AFVs for most of their anti-aircraft missiles. All three of the above systems are organised into battalions of 18 vehicles, six to a battery, and in action are deployed, just like conventional Soviet artillery, in straight lines in the open — making them rather vulnerable to enemy fire.

Above: An artist's impression of the Soviet 220mm BM-27 Rocket System, which fires a salvo of 16 HE rockets.

TANK BUSTERS

FH70

The FH70 project originated in 1968 when Britain and West Germany signed a collaboration agreement to design and produce a new 155mm towed howitzer; Italy joined the project in 1970 and the first battery of six guns commenced trials in 1975. Prime contractors were the Royal Armament Research and Development Establishment, Vickers-Armstrong, Royal Ordnance Factories, and Rheinmetall, with various Italian firms including OTO-Melara being involved in sub-assembly construction. The result has been a technologically advanced weapon of great capabilities able to fire all standard NATO 155mm rounds at ranges up to 18 miles (30km), including SADARM in due course.

FH70 is a large gun with a barrel length of 19.8ft (6.04m), the barrel with its large muzzle brake being reversed over the split trails for towing, and is normally crewed by eight men. A most unusual feature of the gun is the auxiliary VW 76bhp petrol engine which drives the two main wheels, two dolly wheels being attached to the ends of the trails. This was considered necessary because the gun is too heavy at 20,162lb (9,144kg) to manhandle over anything except the shortest distances.

In action the wheels are raised and the front of the gun rests upon a firing platform which gives exceptional stability and thus accuracy; there are also two recoil spades at the end of the trails. The buffer and recuperator are fitted below the barrel and the breech block is similar to that of the Rheinmetall gun fitted to the M109. A self-propelled variant of FH70, designated SP70, is under development.

Right: An FH70 during firing trials in Italy. Note the dolly wheel on the ends of the trails.

Below: Behind this FH70, whose small auxiliary Volkswagen engine is on the front of the carriage, is a Foden FH70 gun limber with palletised ammunition load.

GUNS, ARTILLERY, ARTILLERY ROCKETS

TANK BUSTERS

Multiple Launch Rocket System (MLRS)

After protracted development since 1972, MLRS first entered US Army service in 1983 and is also being purchased by Britain, France, Italy and West Germany. Designed to supplement but not replace conventional artillery such as the M110 8in (203mm) SPH, MLRS will be a major area denial weapon in any future European conflict and has a significant anti-tank capability. The carrier vehicle is a much-modified M2 Bradley with an armoured crew cab at the front and launch tubes for 12 solid-fuel missiles at the rear. These 600lb (272kg) rockets have a range of over 18 miles (30km) and can be fired singly or in ripple salvoes. The warhead contains a variety of submunitions, the most important of which, in the anti-armour role, will be the new Sense and Destroy Armour (SADARM) round. This comprises a cargo body with a sensor in its nose to detect enemy tanks, a fuze and six Skeet submunitions. When enemy armour is detected the fuze explodes, releasing the Skeets which descend spinning towards the target area, scanning with IR detectors. At a pre-determined height above a target vehicle the explosively forged projectile (EFP) fires itself at a high but undisclosed velocity and will penetrate the top armour of all known AFVs. If the Skeet fails to find a target it turns itself into a mine which will similarly penetrate the bottom armour of any current tank. Other submunitions which can be fired by MLRS include no fewer than 644 M77 hollow-charge minelets capable of penetrating 4in (100mm) of armour.

The carrier vehicle, with its crew of three or four, is designed to be able to keep up with MBTs in accordance with the latest NATO tactical doctrine of taking a hard offensive against a Soviet attack and carrying the battle into enemy territory. It has a top road speed of 40mph (64km/h) and a range of 300 miles (483km), and, being tracked, has good cross-country mobility. Each MLRS will be accompanied by one or two missile resupply vehicles.

GUNS, ARTILLERY, ARTILLERY ROCKETS

Above: An MLRS on loan to the British Army for trials. The rocket launcher traverses through 180° to acquire a target.

Below: The launch of an MLRS rocket is nothing if not dramatic. They would normally be fired in a ripple salvo.

Anti-tank Mines

THE ANTI-TANK mine is a potent weapon and one of the tank's greatest enemies. The basic anti-tank mine is a simple metal container packed with explosive and activated by a pressure or mast fuze, but over the last few years this classic form has been much altered by three things: the advent of non-metallic components, the need for rapid laying, and the increasing use of electronic sensors for fuzing.

Non-metallic materials have been introduced to prevent mines being detonated by magnetic sensor devices such as hand-held mine detectors. Many mines now use plastic or nylon-based containers, and their fuzes often contain little, if any, metal. The use of these non-metallic materials also has the advantage that the mines can withstand rough handling and laying methods.

The need for rapid laying is an offshoot of the anticipated mobile warfare that is likely to occur in any future conflict. Minefields will have to be produced quickly in the path of advancing enemy forces, and various mechanical minelaying methods have been developed. The most rapid methods have been developed for helicopters, ranging from simply dropping mines from a suspended crate to dispensing them via a chute secured to a hatch. Other more advanced methods include firing mines from dispenser tubes to cover large areas. Typical of the latter are the American Volcano and the West German Minenwerfersystem (MiWS). The MiWS also has a ground component carried on tracked vehicles. As the carrier vehicle advances the dispenser tubes are fired at pre-selected intervals to scatter small anti-tank mines over a large area.

Other methods of laying include towed or motorised ploughs that actually bury anti-tank mines below the surface. On most of these systems, including the British Bar Mine system, mines are inserted down a chute and as the plough moves forward the mines are buried at selected intervals. Other rapid-scattering ▶

Anti-tank mines

Name	Origin	Overall weight lb(kg)
ACPM (light)	France	13.89 (6.30)
ACPM (heavy)	France	18.74 (8.50)
Barmine	UK	24.25 (11.00)
C-3-A	Spain	13.01 (5.90)
FFV 028	Sweden	17.42 (7.90)
HCT	Italy	8.82 (4.00)
HPD-1	France	13.23 (6.00)
M15	USA	31.46 (14.27)
M19	USA	27.69 (12.56)
M21	USA	17.42 (7.90)
M66	USA	17.99 (8.16)
M75 (GEMSS/RAAMS)	USA	3.70 (1.68)
M77	USA	0.51 (0.23)
Mark 7	UK	30.00 (13.60)
MiWS AT2	W. Germany	4.87 (2.21)
Panzermine 75	Austria	18.08 (8.20)
PM83	Austria	16.54 (7.50)
PM3000	Austria	17.64 (8.00)
SB-81	Italy	7.05 (3.20)
TM-46	USSR	18.52 (8.40)
TM-62M	USSR	21.28 (9.65)
Type 72	China	14.33 (6.50)
WASPM	USA	34.99 (15.87)

Whether air-dropped or laid conventionally, the mine can still cripple the heaviest of tanks.

Charge weight lb(kg)	Diameter in(mm)	Length in(mm)	Width in(mm)	Height in(mm)	Armour penetration in(mm)
8.82 (4.00)	–	11.02 (280)	7.28 (185)	4.13 (105)	2.75 (70)
13.23 (6.00)	–	11.02 (280)	9.92 (252)	4.13 (105)	n/a
15.88 (7.2)	–	47.24 (1,200)	42.52 (1,080)	3.19 (81)	n/a
11.02 (5.00)	11.22 (285)	–	–	4.53 (115)	n/a
8.38 (3.8)	9.84 (250)	–	–	4.33 (110)	2.75 (70)
4.52 (2.05)	8.74 (222)	–	–	4.33 (110)	6.89+ (175+)
8.82 (4.00)	–	11.02 (280)	7.28 (185)	4.13 (105)	2.75 (70)
22.78 (10.33)	13.27 (337)	–	–	4.92 (125)	n/a
21.01 (9.53)	–	13.00 (330)	13.07 (332)	3.70 (94)	n/a
10.80 (4.90)	9.05 (230)	–	–	8.11 (206)	n/a
1.88 (0.85)	–	23.98 (609)	3.50 (89)	3.50 (89)	3.94 (100)
n/a	4.68 (119)	–	–	2.60 (66)	Causes damage to tracks only
n/a	n/a	n/a	n/a	n/a	3.94 (100)
19.60 (8.89)	12.79 (325)	–	–	5.12 (130)	n/a
n/a	4.05 (103)	–	–	5.04 (128)	5.51 (140)
16.32 (7.40)	–	11.02 (280)	11.02 (280)	4.72 (120)	n/a
8.82 (4.00)	–	11.02 (280)	11.02 (280)	5.51 (140)	2.36 (60)
n/a	–	11.02 (280)	11.02 (280)	3.94 (100)	7.09 (180)
4.41 (2.00)	9.13 (232)	–	–	3.54 (90)	3.94+ (100+)
11.69 (5.30)	11.97 (304)	–	–	3.58 (91)	n/a
15.43 (7.00)	12.52 (318)	–	–	4.41 (112)	n/a
11.91 (5.40)	10.63 (270)	–	–	3.94 (100)	n/a
EFP	10.98 (279)	–	–	15.00 (381)	Effective against MBT side armour

▶ devices include the American M128 'Frisbee Flinger' that hurls mines from a rotating arm. Artillery is now used to fire shells carrying small anti-tank arms that are dispensed while the shell is still in flight — artillery rockets are also used in this manner.

Electronic sensors now make the anti-tank mine a very versatile weapon. All manner of sensors can be employed, ranging from simple pressure fuzes to devices that operate using IR, seismic, acoustic, magnetic or other inputs — sometimes fuzes with sensor combinations (e.g. pressure and acoustic) are used. These sensors can be very sophisticated, allowing the mines to be detonated only when tracked, rather than wheeled, vehicles pass nearby, and some incorporate counters or pressure detectors that operate only when a number of targets have passed.

Electronic circuits can also be incorporated to detonate the mine after a pre-selected time or else neutralise it so that the mine can be lifted and reused somewhere else. Either of these ploys reduces the need for dangerous and time-consuming clearing operations. Technology now permits these electronic fuzes to be fitted to older types of anti-tank mine to update stocks of otherwise obsolescent mines. The relatively cheap and simple course of adapting elderly pressure fuzes to operate using mast sensors (that detonate the mine when they are bent or snapped off when a tank passes over them) can ensure that the mine detonates right under the tank and thus produces the maximum blast damage against the relatively thin underbelly armour of the tank.

Anti-tank mines frequently use hollow-charge or self-forging fragment warheads for armour penetration and only rarely rely on blast alone. Some types of buried mine use a small charge to remove soil or other cover from over the mine warhead before the main hollow-charge or self-forging fragment warhead is fired — this ensures the maximum on-target efficiency.

Special mines that are fired into the side armour of vehicles have also been developed. These are usually placed on some form of stand in ambush locations and are fired automatically as a tank passes. The fuzes can be electronic sensors but usually some form of pressure tape is used actually to fire the mine. A recent innovation is the coupling of electronic sensors to infantry anti-tank projectors to create 'stand alone' side-attack anti-tank mines. These side-attack mines are frequently placed on the approaches to minefields for use against mine-clearing vehicles.

Anti-tank Grenades

The anti-tank grenade is becoming an obsolete weapon because only very large explosive charges can inflict viable damage on the thick armour of many modern tanks. However, the small anti-tank grenade can be used against lightly armoured vehicles, and even against large ones a well-placed grenade can damage vision devices, damage tracks, or blow off radio aerials, all of which can reduce a tank's effectiveness in combat.

The hand-thrown anti-tank grenade is now a combat rarity. Some, such as the Soviet RPG-6 or RPG-43, are still encountered in the hands of guerrillas or 'freedom fighters' but the most common form of anti-tank grenade is now the rifle grenade. Propelled by special cartridges or simply by firing a bullet into the body of a grenade placed over a rifle muzzle, these weapons can have a range of hundreds of yards. At such ranges they are inaccurate unless used with complicated sighting devices.

For some reason Belgium produces more anti-tank grenades than any other nation. Mecar and Fabrique Nationale (FN) produce a range of grenades, nearly all with small hollow-charge warheads that can be adapted to suit almost any combat rifle or calibre in use. They all use tail fins for flight stabilisation to ensure the warhead strikes the target head-on, but the actual damage inflicted is usually limited by the small warhead diameters involved, 2.3in (58mm) being about the maximum. Such grenades provide the foot soldier with limited anti-armour capability, but they can knock out light AFVs.

Glossary

AA	anti-aircraft
AALAAW	Advanced Air-launched Anti-Armour Weapon
ABOL	all-burnt on launch
AFRes	Air Force Reserve
AFV	armoured fighting vehicle
ANG	Air National Guard
AP	armour-piercing
APC i	armoured personnel carrier
APC ii	armour-piercing capped
APDS	armour-piercing discarding sabot
APERS-T	anti-personnel tracer
APFSDS	armour-piercing fin-stabilised discarding sabot
APHE	armour-piercing high-explosive
ApILAS	Armour-Piercing Infantry Light Arm System
AT	anti-tank
ATGW	anti-tank guided weapon
BAOR	British Army of the Rhine
BILL	Bofors, Infantry, Light and Lethal
CBU	cluster bomb unit
CCIP	continuously computed impact point
CVRT	Combat Vehicle Reconnaissance (Tracked)
ECM	electronic counter-measures
EFP	explosively forged projectile
EMP	electro-magnetic pulse
EO	electro-optical
ERAM	Extended Range Anti-Armour Munition
ERW	Enhanced Radiation Weapon
FAE	fuel-air explosive
FLOT	front line of troops
HC	hollow-charge
HE	high-explosive
HEAT	high-explosive anti-tank
HESH	high-explosive squash-head
HOT	*haut subsonique optiquement téléguide d'un tube*
HUD	head-up display
HVAPDS	high-velocity armour-piercing discarding sabot
HVM	Hyper-Velocity Missile
IDF	Israeli Defence Forces
IFCS	integrated fire-control system
IFF	identification friend or foe
IFV	infantry fighting vehicle
IIR	imaging infra-red
IR	infra-red
KEP	kinetic energy penetrator
LAD	Low-Altitude Dispenser
LANTIRN	low-altitude navigation and targeting infra-red system
LAW	light anti-armour weapon
LGB	laser-guided bomb
LLLGB	Low-Level Laser-Guided Bomb
LOS	line-of-sight
MAW	medium anti-armour weapon
MBT	main battle tank
MCLOS	manual command to line-of-sight
MICV	mechanised infantry combat vehicle
MILAN	*missile infanterie légère anti-char*
MLRS	Multiple Launch Rocket System
NBC	nuclear, biological, chemical
NOE	nap-of-the-earth
PLSS	Precision Location Strike System
RAAMS	Remote Anti-Armour Mine System
RPV	remotely piloted vehicle
SACLOS	semi-automatic command to line-of-sight
SADARM	Sense-And-Destroy Armour
SAM	surface-to-air missile
SPG	self-propelled gun
SPH	self-propelled howitzer
STARS	Surveillance Target Attack Radar System
TOW	tube-launched, optically-tracked, wire-guided
VIRRS	Visual and Infra-Red Smoke

OTHER SUPER-VALUE GUIDES IN THIS SERIES...

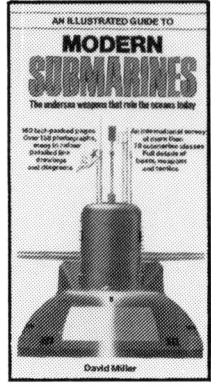

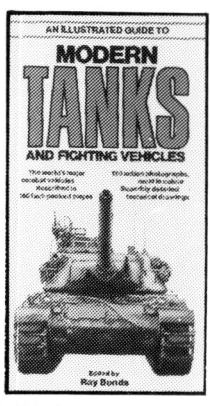

OTHER ILLUSTRATED MILITARY GUIDES NOW AVAILABLE...

Rifles and Sub-Machine Guns
Pistols and Revolvers
Bombers of World War II
Military Helicopters
Modern Soviet Air Force
Modern US Air Force
Modern Warships
Soviet Ground Forces

★ Each has 160 fact-filled pages
★ Each is colourfully illustrated with hundreds of action photographs and technical drawings
★ Each contains concisely presented data and accurate descriptions of major international weapons
★ Each represents tremendous value

Further titles in this series are in preparation
Your military library will be incomplete without them.